Making It Personal

Also by Leslie Linsley

Custom-Made

Fabulous Furniture Decorations

Wildcrafts

The Decoupage Workshop

Scrimshaw

Decoupage: A New Look at an Old Craft

Decoupage for Young Crafters

Decoupage On . . .

Army/Navy Surplus: A Source of Decorating Ideas

Photocraft

New Ideas for Old Furniture

The Great Bazaar

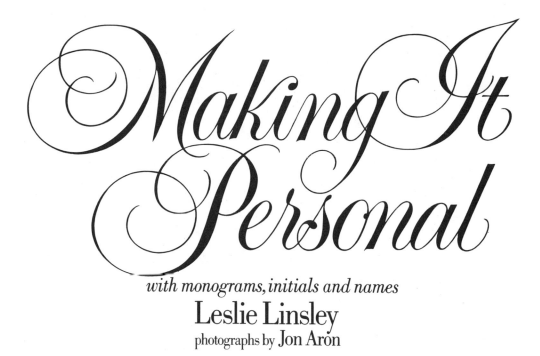

Making It Personal

with monograms, initials and names

Leslie Linsley

photographs by Jon Aron

Richard Marek Publishers
New York

Acknowledgments

The projects on pages 39, 43, 61, 65, 80, 82 and 130 were worked by Elizabeth Gilbert, who owns the Craft Center (for needlework supplies, custom designs and accessories), Nantucket, Massachusetts 02554.

The projects on pages 64, 69, 157 and 169 were worked by Christine Bartlett.

Grateful acknowledgment goes also to my mother, Ruth Linsley, who contributed her crafting expertise to many of the projects presented in the book.

All wallcover used in the crafting projects or in the finished photographs is from Wall-Tex by the Borden Company.

Library of Congress Cataloging in Publication Data

Linsley, Leslie.
   Making it personal with monograms, initials, and names.

   1. Needlework. 2. Alphabets. 3. Initials.
4. Monograms. I. Title.
TT751.L52   746.4   81-3739
ISBN 0-399-90125-6   AACR2

Designed by Jon Aron

Printed in the United States of America

Contents

Contents

Contents

Alphabet locator

Making It Personal

Personalizing your crafts

Crafts are once again on the rise after a few slow years when most of us were busy bringing up children, developing careers and buying more accessories than we were making. Although we still lack time, our desire for some personal statement when everything seems so impersonal has led us back to crafting. But now people are more demanding and specific about where they will put their time and efforts.

Over the past twelve years my husband/partner, Jon Aron, and I have designed hundreds of projects for more than a dozen books and many magazines. We have designed kits as well. It has been important for us to be aware of what our audience, crafters of all ages from all over the country, is looking for in a craft project. It used to be important to design projects for lengthy crafting techniques that involved many detailed instructions and how-to photos. In the past couple of years the letters we receive and the research we do have indicated changes in people's life-styles and consequently in needs and tastes. In the beginning, when there were many, many new crafts introduced yearly, the detailed instructions were necessary. Now almost everyone has some knowledge of a variety of crafts and has become savvy about using materials that were once unknown. Also, with so many techniques on the market, people don't want to limit themselves to one craft. Because of the lack of time and often space, crafting that takes a long time to master or requires large and expensive equipment is no longer as desirable as it once was. However, we have become more sophisticated as we have been exposed to more and more well-designed items, and we aren't willing to compromise with our tastes.

The message Jon and I hear is that people who do crafts are hungry for design ideas to apply to familiar, useful or decorative projects. And the single, most popular design application in any technique is one that is personalized. Whenever we design a project that is monogrammed the response is overwhelmingly positive.

There are two basic reasons for doing a personalized craft project: to serve one's own use or to serve as a gift. Further, when we add initials to an item, we create a keepsake or something that may become an heirloom. Store-bought personalized items are extremely expensive, yet personalizing is the very thing that makes a gift special. By taking everyday items, designing them in a pretty way and adding the personal touch of a name or initial, we have an appealing reason for making the items. The personalizing aspect of these craft projects is in keeping with the reason for making them in the first place. The gift then becomes everlasting.

You will find dozens of patterns and a variety of alphabets that we've selected and created to be applied to these projects. The designs and alphabets are quite versatile and can be used on other projects, or you can use an alphabet from one project with a design from another. You will also find a section on personalizing purchased items for those who want to do only the decorations or trimmings, not the crafting.

The following section will tell you something about the alphabets and how they are used on the projects. Jon Aron is a typographic designer and has carefully selected the alphabets that go best with each project.

Leslie Linsley

A note about the alphabets

Personalizing is an excellent way to solve most problems of what design to use on a craft project. It does two things: It is decorative, and it gives the project relevance. For example, embroidering a napkin with a pretty floral design is a nice project. Add a monogram to the design, and it takes on another dimension. The project and the design become part of the person who owns it.

The basic way to make something personal is with initials, monograms (combinations of two or more initials of a person's name to form one design) and names.

The alphabets presented here are a combination of typefaces used in printing and original hand-drawn alphabets made exclusively for this book. The hand-drawn alphabets were developed for use as monograms because few typefaces exist for this purpose.

Alphabets reflect the period and environment in which they are developed and used. Like clothing and automobiles, they are a reflection of fashion. All the projects offered here take this into consideration and incorporate the "personality" of the alphabet into the overall feeling of the project. For example, Alphabet 27 is a florid Victorian typeface. The decorations are quite ornate. This alphabet, called Lady Text, is used to decorate a lacy evening bag (see page 162). The effect is Victoriana all the way.

Typefaces are not discarded when they go out of fashion. They just sit in their typecases year after year until someone decides they are so far out of fashion that they must be in fashion. As a result, alphabets from other periods are common and popular today.

Art Nouveau and Art Deco styles in art and

decorating have counterparts in alphabets. Art Nouveau alphabets tend to be squiggly and full of twists and curves. Like Alphabets 1, 2 and 12, they all seem to have a sense of humor built into them. Because of their intricacy, they are good initials for embroidery.

Scripts are the traditional alphabets used for initialing and monogramming. Their graceful curves have always attracted designers and crafters. There are four different scripts used in this book: 13, a very delicate formal script; 3, a bolder formal script; 28, a unique alphabet that combines the qualities of script lettering with the flair of personal handwriting; 21, an Art Nouveau script alphabet that is casual and highly decorative.

Alphabet 14 is charted for needlepoint and therefore slightly modified from its original use on nineteenth-century American posters that decorated store windows and proclaimed "Reward Dead or Alive" in hundreds of cowboy movies. This, and Alphabet 25, are typical American wood types of alphabets. Their simplicity and directness are qualities to take advantage of. The coasters on pages 80 and 82 and the bookmark on page 82 are designed in bold poster style.

Alphabet 4 is a classical Roman alphabet with each leg standing securely on a serif. This alphabet is particularly good for initials or monograms that are formal, symmetrical and elegant. See pages 42 and 123 for projects using this alphabet.

Serifs are residual design elements left over from the original inspirations, which were letters chiseled into stone by artisans living centuries ago. Many modern alphabets have no serifs and

Alphabet 2

Alphabet 12

Alphabet 13

Alphabet 3

Alphabet 21

Alphabet 4

Alphabet 14

Alphabet 25

Alphabet 17
Alphabet 20
Alphabet 5
Alphabet 15
Alphabet 23
Alphabet 18
Alphabet 9
Alphabet 7

are called sans serif or block letters. They are lean and modern-looking. They go with contemporary design that is unadorned or geometric, like the projects on pages 97, 130 and 140.

Alphabet 5 was developed for use on casual projects and for children's items. It is easy to use and can be copied freehand after a few words have been traced.

Stencil alphabets come in many styles. The stencil used on the child's apron (page 113) is a dime-store variety, charmingly familiar. On the other hand, Alphabet 15, which is drawn from metal Corbu stencils, is sophisticated and quite popular with architects and designers. It lends an elegance to the fun that is part of the quality of the country tote (page 147), the children's boots (page 138) and the sundress (page 106).

The cross-stitch Alphabet 23 is good for large, simple projects. Only the lower case is provided because it is designed for use on modern designs like the lap napkins (page 143). The other cross-stitch alphabet, 18, is a script that can be used for samples, name plaques and decorative projects like the ones on pages 116 and 118.

The tablecloth on page 46 is a reminder that there are many ways to express your personality, including signing your name. Experiment with different ideas presented here to find the methods that suit you.

Jon Aron

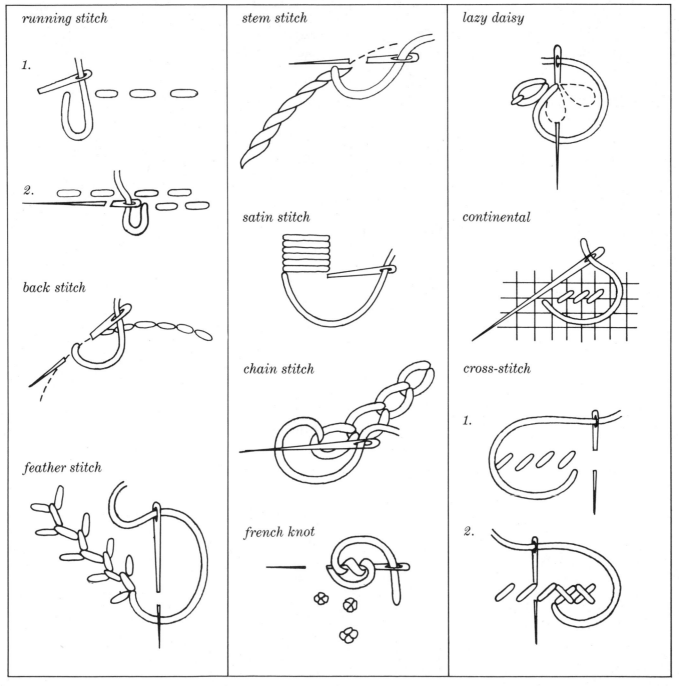

running stitch

1.

2.

back stitch

feather stitch

stem stitch

satin stitch

chain stitch

french knot

lazy daisy

continental

cross-stitch

1.

2.

General crafting information

The following are brief introductions to general crafting techniques that are used on the projects in this book. They are summarized for easy referral as you work on a specific project.

Embroidery

Embroidery is like painting with a needle and thread. It is the application of stitches to fabric in order to create a decoration. There are many different stitches, and each is designed to either outline or fill in a selected design or illustration.

Embroidery is a traditional method for decorating a variety of personal apparel, such as a dainty handkerchief, a slip, the collar on a blouse, or home accessories, like tablecloths and napkins, bedspreads and pillows. Sometimes the stitches simply add a decorative border to an otherwise plain item. Or you may find a framed illustration that is elaborately worked. The beauty of embroidery is that the stitches are not difficult to learn, the design possibilities are quite extensive and the potential for creative expression is unlimited.

Fabrics

Almost any fabric can be used for embroidery; however, some fabrics produce better results than others. Cotton and even-weave linen are most often used. The loosely woven fabrics are less desirable. Velvet and terry cloth are generally difficult to work on. A delicate fabric, such as silk or organdy, must be stitched more carefully than a plain basket-weave fabric.

If you are painting on fabric, the smoother, tighter weaves will provide the best results. If you are using textile markers, be sure to test the material on the underside to see how it takes the marker.

Designs

What design do you embroider? Many fabrics are commercially printed with a design to be embroidered. This, however, limits you in fabric, design and size. With the new techniques and materials available, almost any design can be transferred to the fabric of your choice.

When you select a design, consider first the item you will be working on. The design should be appropriate, whether it is a decorative border, a bouquet of flowers or a monogram. The next consideration is placement. Where on the item should the design be placed? The size of the design should relate to the size of the item. If the design you select can be used in its original size, it will be easy to transfer. If you want to enlarge the size, you can use the grid method described below. The design is then transferred in an appropriate way for the specific design and material you are using.

Enlarging designs and patterns

Many of the designs provided here may not be the exact size for your project. They have been reduced in order to fit into the book. You may find an appealing design that is just right for the item you are making but feel that it should be larger. This is not a problem. Some designs appear on grids, but it is often difficult to show the details and markings of a sewing pattern, for example, with small squares over it. In this case you will have to make a grid over it before enlarging.

For some designs shown on a grid there is an indication of the size each square represents. For example, one square may equal 1 inch; that means you will transfer or copy the design to graph paper marked with 1-inch squares. Pads

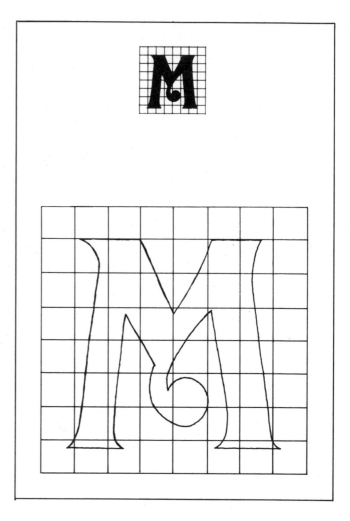

Opposite: Tape design under sheer fabric, and trace over with a soft pencil.

or sheets of graph paper are available in art supply and needlework stores. The back of self-adhesive paper, such as Con-Tact, is divided into 1-inch squares which are easy to use because the lines are boldly marked.

Begin by counting the horizontal and vertical rows of squares on the design in the book. Count the same number of rows on the larger graph. Copy the design onto your grid one square at a time. For difficult designs, mark each grid line with a dot where it is intersected by the design. Then connect the dots, following the contour of the original.

Transferring designs

There are several methods for transferring designs to fabric. The easiest to use is a full-color *hot-iron transfer* that has been preprinted on a special paper. You simply place the design face-down on the desired area of your fabric and press with a hot iron. Lift the paper, and the design is transferred with a clear outline on your fabric. When you stitch, you must cover the transfer lines with the threads. This method limits you to those designs which have been printed for this purpose and eliminates the possiblities of any original design.

Using Pressure-Fax pen, trace design on special paper supplied with pen.

Dressmaker's carbon is different from type-writer carbon paper. It comes in light and dark colors to accommodate your fabric. Trace the desired design onto tracing paper. Position the tracing over the fabric, and use masking tape to secure it in place. Slip a piece of carbon (face-down) between the fabric and tracing paper. Outline the tracing with a pencil, pressing down in order to transfer the design. With this method you can use any illustration you find. You are not limited to what has already been made specifi-cally for embroidery.

Transfer pencil or crayon is yet another method to use. Most notions stores sell this product. First you draw or trace a design with the transfer pencil. Place the tracing paper with the drawing side down on the fabric, and press it with a medium-hot iron. The design will be reversed on the fabric, so if you are transferring an initial or a number, plan accordingly.

Washable marker can be applied right to the fabric and the marks can be easily removed with plain water. Draw or trace directly onto your fabric. Work the stitches. When you are finished, remove the markings by rubbing them gently with a damp cloth. This relatively new product can be found in needlework shops.

Pressure-Fax is a kit that comes with a special transfer pen and paper; it is available in notions and art needlework stores. Trace a design on regular tracing paper. Tape or pin the tracing over the Pressure-Fax paper, and retrace with the pen. Work from the center of the design toward the outer lines to avoid smudging the ink. If you are creating names and initials or num-bers, trace the design, turn it over onto the

22

Burnish design from paper to fabric.

Remove transfer paper.

transfer paper and retrace with the transfer pen. It will appear backwards.

Next, place the transfer paper facedown over your fabric, and tape or pin them together. With the back of a spoon, your fingernail or any other hard surface, rub over the entire transfer. Lift a corner of the paper to see if the design has taken on the fabric. If some areas are light, go over them with more pressure.

I have found this last method to be the easiest and most accurate. However, you must take extra care with some fabrics to avoid bleeding of the ink. Further, with this method you must wait for the ink to dry before you proceed. This might take from one to four hours. However, if you apply the design to your fabric the day before you begin, you won't have any difficulty with the product.

When you are working on a fabric, such as velvet or terry cloth, that won't take a transfer, the *organdy appliqué* method can be used: trace the chosen design onto a sheer piece of organdy or Stitch Witchery (sold by the yard in fabric shops). Baste this to the front of the fabric. Embroider right through the two fabrics. Remove the fabric (organdy or Stitch Witchery) with the design by clipping away excess material. Pull the excess threads away with a tweezer.

Materials and tools for embroidery

An embroidery hoop is a must for almost all your projects. If the area to be stitched is taut, the work will not pucker or become misshapen. When you set the work aside, always remove the hoop so there is no permanent crease on the material.

Embroidery floss comes in almost every shade of every color imaginable. The floss comes in six strands, and some of your projects will be stitched with all six, some with only two or three. The number will depend on the weight of the fabric, the delicacy or boldness of the design and the type of stitch used.

A thimble is a handy tool. It will add to the comfort and ease with which you do your sewing. Small, sharp scissors should be kept at hand when you do any needlework. A magnifying glass is indispensable for fine work.

Stitches

Most of the stitches used for the projects here are the basic embroidery stitches. Many of the designs can be adapted for more elaborate work depending on your needlework skills and the time you want to spend on a project.

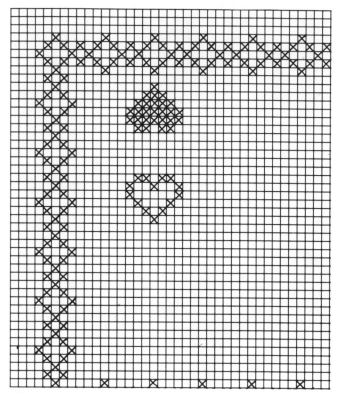

Charted design for counted cross-stitch.

Cross-stitch

Some of the projects employ the versatile cross-stitch. It is the most popular stitch used today. If you are a beginner, you might try the easiest method for transferring a design. (See page 120 for a variety of cross-stitch designs.) If you use gingham or a similar checked material, your cross-stitch will be perfect. The size of your finished design will depend on the size of the checks in the fabric. You won't have to transfer the pattern; just copy the charted design square by square.

Any even-weave fabric, such as linen, Hardanger or Aida cloth (available in needle art

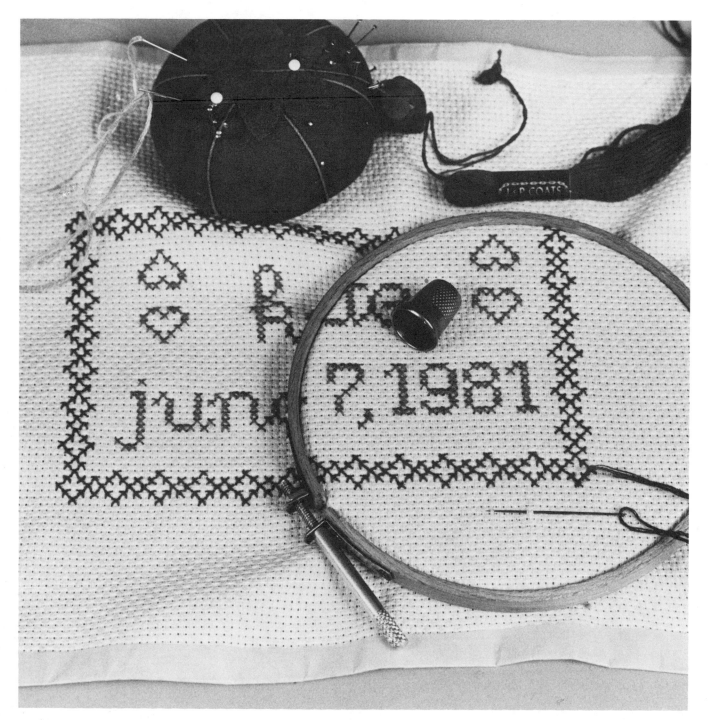

shops), can be successfully used if you count the threads for placement of the stitches.

Cross-stitch is, as its name implies, an *X* which, when placed in a series according to a charted pattern, creates a neat, crisp motif. Many early American samplers employ the basic cross-stitch. The best way to work it is by stitching all lines slanted in one direction and then the other. All top threads must cross over in the same direction.

Appliqué

Pieces of fabric that are sewn to a large piece of fabric in order to create a design are called appliqué. The appliqué can be attached by hand or sewing machine. Another easy method utilizes a thin, fusible web that is sandwiched between both pieces of material. They are fused together with an iron set at the temperature for the material. The edges can then be machine stitched or left as is if the appliqué is small.

Appliqué label for little carpenter's apron page 111

If you are cutting out more than one appliqué of the same size, a template should be used. Transfer your traced pattern onto a piece of shirt cardboard or the back of a piece of sandpaper. This will keep the template from slipping as you trace around it on slippery material like satin (good for appliqués). Do not allow extra for seams. Use the template to trace as many appliqués as needed for your project.

If you are not creating your own appliqué shapes, you can cut out designs from sheets or other printed fabric. For example, you might cut large colorful flowers from one material to apply to the front of a vest (see page 125) or a bird from another fabric to apply to the front of a shirt (see page 127).

Quilting

Quilting is the stitching together of two pieces of fabric with a layer of filler sandwiched between. It can be done by hand or machine, the choice often determined by the size of the project. It can also be done with large, solid pieces of fabric or with small pieces of fabric stitched together, which is called patchwork.

The filler or interlining used for quilting is called batting. This is made of Dacron or cotton. It comes in sheet form, which is best for quilt making, or loose and resembling a giant cotton ball from which you pull off as much as you need. Loose filler is often used for pillows because it creates a puffy effect.

Borders

The quilt border is like a frame for the design contained in the center of the major section of the quilt. It is often made of a contrasting color that doesn't detract from the design. (See reversible crib quilt on page 97.)

Fabric painting

This is a fast and easy way to create designs that often look like thread embroidery. Colorfast ball-point textile paint tubes are available in art supply and fabric stores (one brand name is Vogart). You use the tubes as you would a marker, and the various colors give you flexibility of shading and design. They are permanent once applied. (See page 147.)

Fabric crayons require a different method for applying but are also easy to work with. First you draw a design on paper. Color it in as you would a drawing in a coloring book. No special skills are required. The crayon picture is then placed facedown on the fabric and transferred with a hot iron. The results are like a pastel watercolor painting. (See page 113.)

Acrylic paint is used for stenciling on fabric. It is water-soluble but permanent once applied to fabric. It also comes in a wide range of colors, unlike the crayons or fabric tubes.

Felt-tip markers are made specially for fabric and are often used on a canvas for needlepoint. Always test the markers on a scrap of material to see the effect. There will be some bleeding when these markers are applied to certain fabrics. Sometimes they don't appear in the exact shade indicated on the tube or you may find that the fabric doesn't "take" the coloring agent.

To ensure a successful design with the use of markers, begin by giving your fabric a light coating of Scotchgard or another fabric protector. This will also retard soiling when the project is in use.

Stenciling

Stenciling is the technique of decorating a surface by applying paint through the perforations in a cutout pattern, or stencil. When the cutout template is removed, the pattern is discernible. This technique is used to decorate walls, floors, furniture and accessories. The projects in this book are limited to small applications utilizing purchased precut stencil letters to form names and initials. You can also buy precut decorative designs, and it is not difficult to cut your own stencils. Simply trace a picture and transfer it to heavy paper such as oak tag or a special waxed paper sold for this purpose. Cut out the design with a sharp X-Acto knife.

Tip: The backing paper that peels away from the Con-Tact and other adhesive paper is excellent for use as a stencil. This backing has a wax coating which enables it to adhere to the surface you will decorate. In this way the paint can't seep under the cutout areas and the outline of your design will be crisp and clearly defined.

Acrylic paint is used for stenciling because it works well on all materials. Although it is water-soluble, it is permanent once applied to fabric. A special stencil brush is available where art supplies are sold.

For the best results always use a dry brush. Dab the stencil brush on the paint. Hold the brush in a vertical position, and tap off excess paint onto a scrap piece of paper before you apply it to your project. (See stencil projects for more detailed directions, pages 106, 138.)

Wrap it up

Many of us find that much of our crafting effort goes toward the making of gifts. Christmas and birthdays give us reason to make things, and our friends and relatives usually look forward to our handmade presents.

I thought it might be fun to offer some creative and coordinated gift wrap ideas to go with each project. You can then be thinking about integrating part of the material, color or theme of your project in the way it is presented. For example, if you are making the bib (page 104) as a gift for a newborn baby, you might save some of the fabric for the outer wrap. The pink embroidery thread can tie the whole thing up, and you can add a matching fabric-backed card.

Each project will contain some specific suggestions for that particular item; however, the following are some general gift wrap ideas.

Some of us feel more comfortable than others wrapping presents. I like to put my creative efforts into making the gifts. Therefore, I usually decide on one theme that will do for all my gifts and really overdo it at holiday time. At Christmas all the presents under my tree look alike. One year I used shiny white shelf paper that is inexpensive and comes on fat rolls from hardware or novelty stores. I bought yards of wide pink satin ribbon and paper doilies to use as medallions and name tags. It made up a romantic and soft theme. Another year road maps were chosen, each package wrapped with a place that had meaning for the recipient. Red ribbons contrasted with the blue map colors.

Another year my daughter wrapped all the packages with pages from magazines. When carefully selected, they create an interesting graphic effect and look like artistic paper.

Some basic materials

Begin by assembling sharp scissors, papers, fabrics, ribbons in various colors and designs, yarn, cellophane tape, tags and stickers, boxes in various sizes to hold your projects.

The basic wrap

The most basic procedure is the wrapping of a square box. Most of us know how to do this with one piece of paper large enough to overlap both ends and meet lengthwise.

If you have a nice box worth keeping, a separately wrapped lid is neat and the box can be used again. Place the lid facedown on a piece of paper that is large enough to be folded up and over the edge of all sides. Tape the two long sides inside the lid. Next, tape the shorter ends inside the lid. Repeat this on the bottom portion of the box. The ribbon can be cut to fit crisscross on the lid and taped to the inside. A separate bow is attached to the top. In this way the top is simply lifted off, keeping the wrapping paper and bow perfectly intact.

Cylinder wrap

When wrapping a cylinder such as a coffee can filled with cookies or a jar filled with potpourri, cut out two circles for the top and bottom. Wrap the package around the middle, and leave a little extra to fold onto the top and bottom. Tape the circles over each end. You can now add a bow to cover the top, or tie ribbons around the middle.

For mailing purposes flat bows are best. Make a flat circle of ribbon, and tape it together. Secure a small piece of ribbon around the middle, and tape it at the back. Use double-faced tape to attach the bow to the package.

Save all scraps of paper, ribbons, fabric, decorative tape, old greeting cards and leftover materials from your projects to make original and personalized gift wraps. When you give a handmade gift, the outer wrap can extend the creative expression and set the stage for the contents.

For special occasions

Special occasions give us one more excuse for crafting. Whether it's making gifts for others or one more set of embroidered napkins with a Christmas design for our own use, nothing gets us going like a coming event. The birth of a new baby is cause for celebration with a gift. A wedding, anniversary, birthday, the first day of spring and certainly Christmas have us reaching into the sewing basket, checking out the new fabrics, looking through the magazines for fresh ideas. It is at these times that we like to give a special gift, set an elegant table, entertain with accessories decorated with the holiday theme.

When we make something for a special occasion that occurs each year, we often like to add to the collection. Such is the case with Christmas tree ornaments. A permanent reminder of a special day can be incorporated in an embroidered birth announcement pillow. A signature tablecloth (page 46) is the kind of lasting gift that brings the person back to the event each time the item is used.

Although all the projects in the book can be adapted for special occasions, the following are designed specifically for the celebrations that we all look forward to and commemorate with gifts.

Luncheon napkin. See design, page 35, and Alphabet 3, page 41.

Luncheon napkins

It's easy to transfer designs to handkerchiefs or cocktail and luncheon napkins made of fine cotton. These are small projects that require only a delicate touch to make them unusual.

To apply the monogram, initial and flowers, begin by tracing the designs (page 35) onto paper (Alphabet 1, page 33). Position and tape the paper to the underside of the fabric. Hold or tape this to a windowpane, and the design will be visible enough to be traced directly onto the material with a light pencil. This method can only be used for thin, light-colored fabric.

Use a simple floral design for the corner of a set of napkins, and if you wish, use the same motif for a tablecloth. Sometimes, as you will see here, the initials are enough of a design without the addition of flowers or other elements. The pretty script letters create their own interwoven pattern, which gives a trademark that makes the project distinctive.

Materials needed

White cotton napkins; tracing paper; pencil; masking tape; pale pink, magenta, light green, darker green and yellow embroidery floss; needle, scissors.

Directions

Trace and transfer the designs to the napkins as suggested above. If you prefer to use an initial design other than the typeface used here, trace and position it with the floral motif. Be sure that the two designs and sizes look good together before they are transferred. You can determine how they will look by tracing the flower design first. Place this tracing over several different alphabets in the book to see how each will look in relation to the flowers. Trace the one that you like best, and transfer it to the napkin.

Use three strands of the light green for leaves and stems, which are done in a satin and running stitch. The accents of the flowers are magenta, and the petals are worked with three strands of pale pink. Use two strands of the darker green floss for the initial, which is done with small running stitches, and, for the heavier lines, done in a satin stitch. A yellow French knot is used for the center of each flower.

Variations

The edges of your napkins might be scalloped and can be finished with white thread or a matching color, such as the pale pink. Try fringing the edge if you prefer not to hem.

The design that you choose will determine the amount of work and time put into the project. If you outline a motif, rather than fill it in, it will take less time. The initial should be appropriately simple.

Gift wrap idea

When you give a set of napkins as a gift, select paper that is designed with the same pastel colors. Use pale green and pale pink ½-inch-wide satin or grosgrain ribbons tied together around a plain white box. Place delicate pink tissue inside to hold the napkins. Transfer the flower design to the front of a plain card, and color it in with markers.

Alphabet 1

33

Art Nouveau napkins

The Art Nouveau designs can be applied to many of the items in the book. These designs lend themselves to embroidery because they're intricate and filled with curves. Nevertheless, this is a simple embroidery project. The color combination you use should match your tablecloth or china.

Materials needed

Linen napkins; tracing paper; pencil; two colors of green embroidery floss; two colors of pink, embroidery hoop, tape, needle, scissors.

Directions

Trace and transfer the design with your initial in position (Alphabet 2, page 36). Embroider the circle with a chain stitch in light green floss. Use light green floss for four rows of backstitch for the wide areas of your initial, tapering it to three rows, two rows and finally one row at the narrow areas. The light green stems and pink flowers are made with a padded satin stitch. The center of flowers and buds is darker pink and the large leaf is dark green.

A B C D E F
G H I J K L
M N O P Q
R S T U V
W X Y Z &

Christmas cheer

Begin the holiday season early by making festive cocktail napkins with a Christmas design. The bow and berry border is created specially to fit on a square napkin. You may want to turn the design so it fits diagonally in one corner. Or enlarge it to fill your napkin. This design can easily be enlarged to fit the center of a tablecloth as well.

Materials needed

Cocktail napkins; tracing paper; masking tape; pencil; red and green embroidery floss; embroidery hoop; needle; scissors.

Directions

Enlarge the design (Alphabet 2, page 36) to fit your napkin. If you are using a white cotton fabric, you can transfer the design with tracing paper and pencil, or trace it right onto the napkin from the book.

Trace the bow and berry border. Position the napkin over the tracing, and tape them together.

Tape this to a windowpane, and retrace the design onto the napkin. Do the same with your initial, which may have to be enlarged to fit the napkin you are using.

Work the embroidery in a hoop, but do not pull threads too tightly. Never knot the thread under your project. Finish off each area by bringing your needle and thread under a few strands of stitches on the underside.

The edges of your napkin can be restitched with red or green embroidery floss if you like.

Variations

If you want to make a set of napkins as a gift, consider using the bow border but eliminating the berries and Christmas colors. Create a pale pink or blue bow with matching initial. You can also add one of the flowers from another project to replace the berries, thus creating your own design. This project makes a lovely wedding, birthday or anniversary gift.

Gift wrap idea

If they are given as a Christmas gift, wrap the napkins with holly berry paper or bright red tissue. Tie the package with a green satin ribbon to match the embroidery thread, and tuck a few sprigs of holly under the bow.

Script and lace

A lace or an embroidered napkin can suggest the style of the monogram to be added. Here a delicate, elegant napkin is enhanced by a beautifully flowing alphabet. The letters are positioned close together and, as with many script letters, may look good overlapping and interlocking each other. This is Alphabet 3.

A monogram is one symbol made from more than one letter. When you look at a monogram, you think not of the individual letters, but rather of the design of all three or two.

Materials needed

Napkin; tracing paper; pencil; embroidery hoop; scissors; blunt needle; embroidery floss; masking tape.

Directions

Trace your initials onto the paper, and position them on the napkin. If you like the way it looks, transfer the design. If you aren't sure, keep retracing your initials so they are spaced differently, or enlarge them to see if the effect is

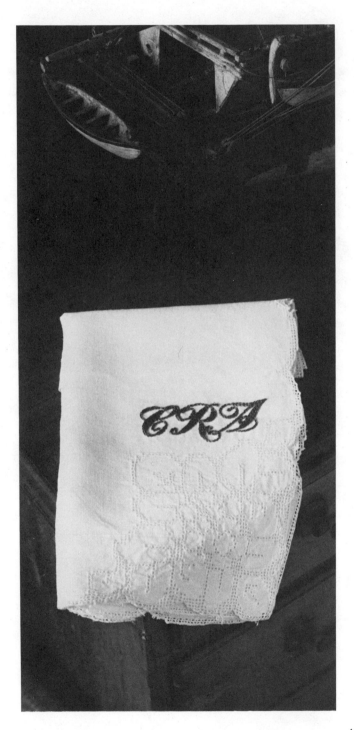

better. Once you have a satisfactory layout, transfer it to one corner of the napkin. It can go across one edge or run up one side or whatever way you think looks best on your napkin.

Use two strands of fine floss, and work the monogram with tiny chain stitches. Use a single row where the lines narrow, two rows where it begins to get wider and three rows of stitches in the widest areas.

Variations

Although this script alphabet is ornamental and stands on its own as a design, you can add flowers, leaves, a butterfly or similar elements to the napkin. Make a tracing of the design, and hold it over the napkin to see how it looks before you transfer it.

Gift wrap idea

Wrap your present with delicately printed paper, and add a doily medallion to the top of the box. Tie with a generous satin bow and again with lace ribbon, creating a double ribbon wrap. Make a small card, and edge it with the lace ribbon.

41

Set a formal table

Nothing makes a holiday table more festive than a delicately embroidered tablecloth. This one belonged to my grandmother, and the white-on-white hand embroidery and cut work are exquisite. When working on an heirloom, choose your design carefully to blend with the existing design of the tablecloth to which it will be applied.

Here a Roman letter is used with an ornamental border designed to go with the formal and delicate quality of the tablecloth. Select light colors if you are not using white on white.

Materials needed

Tablecloth with open area in the center; scissors; wooden embroidery hoop; two pale colors of embroidery floss (fine floss such as DMC is recommended for delicate work); tracing paper; pencil; masking tape; blunt needle; iron; towel.

Directions

You will probably have to enlarge the letter (Alphabet 4, page 45) and border design to suit the size of your cloth. Make a rough sketch on your tracing paper, and position it on the mate-

43

rial to see how it will look. When you think the size is right, make a grid and enlarge the design accordingly. If you have access to a photostat service, have an enlargement made to the exact size needed. (See your Yellow Pages for this service.)

Tape the tracing paper in position, and transfer the design with a pencil. Because the material is delicate, you should have no trouble seeing a pencil outline.

Work with a blunt needle and three strands of fine floss. Here two pastel colors were used in order to show the design, but if you embroider the initial and border with white floss on a white tablecloth, it will be more elegant and formal.

The letter and bow on the border are pale blue, and a stem stitch is used for both. The rest of the border is pale green with the leaves done in a lazy daisy stitch, the stems with a stem stitch and the little lines coming off the stems with a straight stitch.

When you are finished, pad the ironing board with a thick towel. Place the embroidered cloth facedown, and lay a damp cloth over the area to be ironed. Use a dry medium-hot iron.

Variation

The initial can be used by itself on napkins to match the tablecloth. Choose contrasting colors. For example, a light pink or yellow could be used with this green and blue combination. Set the table with pastel candles, and arrange small, individual floral bouquets at each place, leaving the design as the center of attention.

Gift wrap idea

This is the kind of project we usually make for ourselves. However, it can be a really nice wedding present, one that will be kept forever. The wrapping should be as delicate as the item. Use silver or pale blue paper, and transfer the design to the middle of the box. (See page 22 for transfer pencil information.) The blue transfer pencil will make the design seem to have been printed on the paper. Tie a satin ribbon around each corner to set off the design.

Signature tablecloth

Make a keepsake tablecloth that will be a remembrance of a special event for years and years. The petal design is embroidered in the center of the fabric. As the guests arrive at your birthday party or bridal shower, they sign their names within the petals. Later each signature is embroidered. This is an especially nice idea for a shower party because the finished tablecloth can then be given to the couple as a personalized wedding present.

If you want to prepare this as a surprise, simply collect the number of signatures needed on a piece of paper. It's easiest if the names are written large; otherwise you'll have to enlarge them with a grid. (This is not difficult.) Transfer each signature as you would any other design.

Select a solid-color cloth and a pretty print for the underskirt. The printed fabric is also used for the center of the flower. You might get extra printed material for matching napkins.

Materials needed

Solid-color fabric to fit your table; printed fabric for underskirt requiring more yardage; embroidery floss (four skeins for eight petals and border); needle; thread; tracing paper; pencil; masking tape; scissors; iron.

Directions

Enlarge the flower to the desired size on a piece of tracing paper (see page 20). Trace the names in position within each petal on the paper.

Turn the tracing paper over, and go over each line of the signatures and flower with a pencil. Turn the tracing right side up, and tape it to the center of the tablecloth.

Transfer the design by burnishing each line carefully with the closed end of a marker or similar object. Lift a corner of the tracing paper, and carefully check to be sure the transfer is taking to the cloth before you remove it. If the pattern appears light, apply more pressure over the tracing lines.

Turn the hem up on all sides of the tablecloth. Press and slip-stitch.

Finish

A feather stitch is used to decorate the hemline. Place each area to be worked in a wooden embroidery hoop. Vary the embroidery on the signatures by using the stem stitch or backstitch for each one and a chain stitch for the petals. (See stitch guide, page 18.)

Cut a piece of the printed fabric for the center of the flower, and turn the edges. Press and sew to the tablecloth. Trim the edge of the circle with a decorative hand stitch, or use a zigzag on your machine.

Gift wrap idea

When getting signatures, have a large piece of shiny white paper available for everyone to sign with a bright-colored marker. Later use this paper to wrap the gift.

Birthday pillow

Create a permanent record of baby's birthday that will surely become a keepsake for the new mother. This pillow is 11 inches square and would fit nicely into the corner of the crib or carriage. It is an announcement of your baby's name and birth date for all to see.

Cover an existing pillow or make your own. I used part of a blue pillowcase for this project because the cotton was so soft. Select a pale color in soft cotton material. The eyelet border and woven ribbon are separate pieces sewn together. You can select any decorative trim.

This project is made with a blue background and yellow, white and green embroidery; you might select colors that match your baby's room or crib blanket.

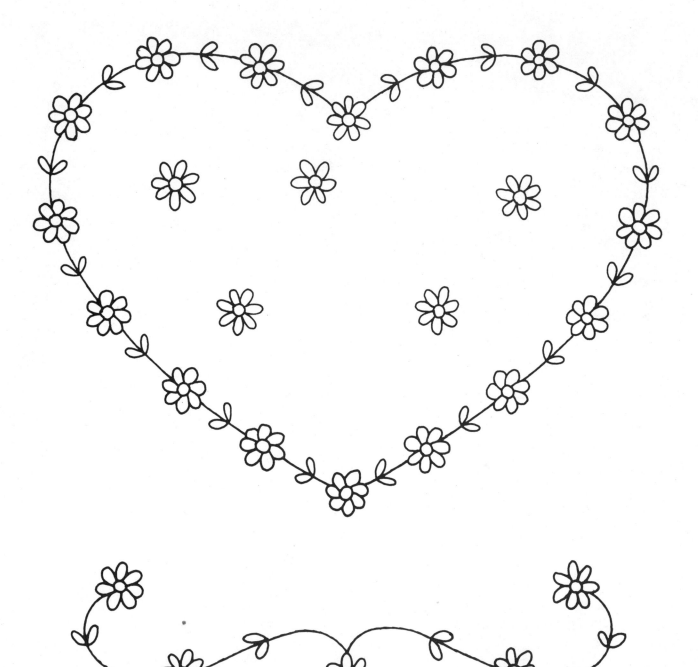

Materials needed

Two pieces of cotton fabric each 12 × 12 inches; 1½ yards 3-inch-wide eyelet; 1½ yards of decorative ribbon; embroidery floss (green, white and yellow used here); needle; tracing paper; pencil; pillow or polyester stuffing; pins; iron; embroidery hoop.

Directions

With right sides together, pin the two pieces of material on three sides. Machine-stitch ¼-inch seams. Turn inside out, and press.

Trace the heart pattern. Find the center of the top of the pillow front. Position the heart approximately 2 inches from the top edge, and transfer it to the fabric.

Using the naïve script Alphabet 5, page 52, trace the name. Turn the paper over, and retrace. Position the name so it is centered in the heart, and transfer it by rubbing over the penciled lines. Trace a few of the flowers, and position them around the name.

Trace, center and transfer the date in the same way. Next, transfer the chain of flowers underneath.

Use an embroidery hoop to create a green chain, white flowers with yellow centers. A running stitch is done in yellow for the letters and numbers. Press it on the wrong side.

Finish

Stuff the pillowcase, or insert the proper size pillow. The excess material on all sides will be pulled taut as the trim is added.

Turn the top opening in to form a finished edge. Press. Pin eyelet trim to the front of the pillow all around the edges. Pin decorative ribbon on top of this to give the edge a finish. Sew close to the pillow edge. Sew the inside edge of the ribbon to the pillowcase. Corners are rounded with the eyelet here, but you can miter them if you desire.

Variation

If you feel ambitious enough to make a matching quilt, this design is easily adaptable. Use the daisy-chain heart in each square, and plan to have the center square hold the name and date. The colors of the quilt can reflect the embroidery colors. Use the eyelet trim all around the edges of the quilt.

To cut down on the work, use the lazy daisy stitch rather than a satin stitch for each petal.

Gift wrap idea

Wrap the pillow with daisy or lacy design paper. Use the decorative ribbon trim on the outer package as well.

a b c d e f g h i j k l m n

o p q r s t u v w x y z

A B C D E F G H I J K

L M N O P Q R S T U

V W X Y Z

1 2 3 4 5 6 7 8 9 10

Baby's bootees

There are several occasions when a little gift for the new baby is appropriate. Make a pair of first bootees for the baby to wear. Or make one bootee with his or her name on the cuff, fill it with a dried flower arrangement and present it to the new mother. A ribbon loop makes it hangable. I especially like one to be used as a first Christmas stocking.

You can buy prequilted fabric, but the selection is limited. It took a few extra minutes to quilt the material I selected, and decorating the cuffs was most enjoyable.

Materials needed

A scrap of material (the bootee measures only 5 inches long and 4 inches at its widest point); small piece of white cotton for the cuff; cotton or polyester batting; scissors; thread; needle; embroidery floss; trimming such as lace and ribbon or rickrack; pins; tracing paper; pencil; iron.

Alphabet 6

stitch line

a b c d e f g h i

j k l m n o p q

r s t u v w x y z

cut ½" larger all around

Directions

Trace the pattern, and cut four for each bootee. Cut two pieces of batting slightly smaller. With right sides to the outside, pin batting between two layers of fabric. Quilt each set by stitching diagonally across the fabric in each direction at 1-inch intervals.

Pin and stitch the front and back sections together with a ¼-inch seam. Leave the top edge open. Turn inside out.

Cut two pieces of white fabric 2½ × 3½ inches for the cuff. Stitch them together on three sides, and turn at the top opening.

Turn the raw edge of bootee down ¼ inch to the inside, and press. Turn the raw edges of the cuff in to create a finished edge. Pin to the top edge of the outside of the bootee. Stitch all around bootee edge.

Add decorative ribbon and lace, and attach a loop at the side for hanging.

Finish

Trace and transfer the name and design (Alphabet 6, page 54) and embroider in the colors to match the fabric. You can also add the birth date if this is to be a gift for a new baby.

Gift wrap idea

Insert a rattle, silver spoon or teething ring into the bootee or on top of the package.

Monograms

Throughout history people have created symbols to represent their families or groups. Coats of arms, family crests, family colors, flags and other insignia are examples. People have applied these devices to their possessions as a matter of identification and a show of family pride.

Today we are more interested in personal identity than in showing our lineage. Nothing is a more personal symbol than a monogram, the device that combines the initials of a person's name into one design element.

Monograms can be designed in many ways. Popular monogram designs include the circle, square and diamond shapes. Many other methods of monogramming are shown in this book as well.

Select a monogram design that appeals to you, and see how many applications would be appropriate for it. You might use the same monogram design on a shirt, towel, tablecloth, tennis racket cover, stationery and scarf.

Your personal monogram, made up from one of the designs in the book, can be used to make a rubber stamp or self-adhesive labels. In this way you will be creating your own trademark.

The techniques used here are primarily embroidery or a form of sewing. Other applications that might be appropriate for the project are fabric painting on an apron, pen and ink on stationery, découpage on a box.

Satin-stitched tablecloth monogram

Monogrammed shirts

The most commonly monogrammed item is a shirt for men and women. Sometimes it is advantageous to do overstitching. When stitching exists on the outside of a garment, you can stitch over it in colors of your choice to create a personal and decorative item.

Consider the shape of the shirt in determining what kind of monogram would look best. Some initials will work better in a circular combination; others, within a diamond shape. A monogram can be made up of two or three initials and can be applied with embroidery thread or fabric markers to the pocket, sleeve or chest area.

Diamond monogram

With a sturdy piece of tracing paper, trace the design backwards, using a straightedge and pencil (Alphabet 7, page 58). Tape the tracing on the shirt in the desired position. Use the top of a pen or marker as a burnisher to transfer the design. Hold the tracing firmly in position while you are burnishing. Check to make sure the design is completely transferred before you remove the tape.

Because this monogram is applied to the front of the pocket, you can't use an embroidery hoop. Hold one hand inside or insert cardboard while working to avoid sewing pocket to shirt. Choose embroidery floss that is slightly darker or lighter than the shade of the material. Because this shirt is made of sheer pink cotton, the work is done with two strands of wine-colored floss.

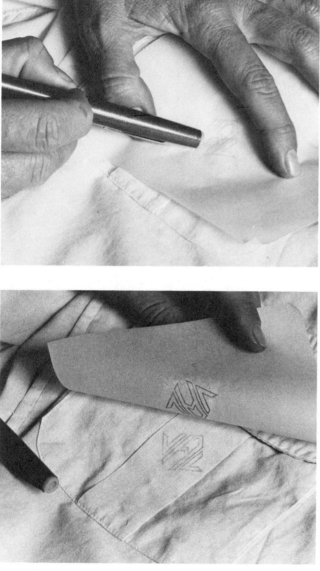

Design colored with marker can be used as is or as a guide for embroidery.

Transfer tip

When you transfer a design by rubbing off the penciled image from tracing paper to a soft fabric, you can prevent the paper from ripping by covering it with transparent tape before you burnish it.

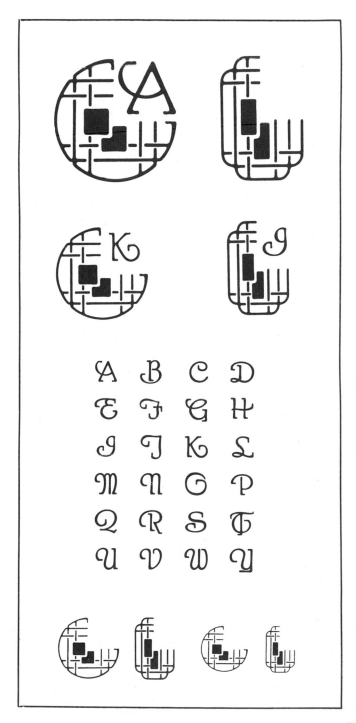

Art Deco monogram

The initial and surrounding design are done in an Art Deco style. The alphabet used here, called Parson's, is number 8, page 60. Choose any of the three designs to combine with your initial, and embroider with two strands, using a very small outline stitch. This is a good way to decorate the corner of a handkerchief, napkins and lingerie. You can adapt it to many of the small projects in the book.

AABBCCDDEE
FJGHHIJJKK
LLMMMMNNOPP
QQRRSSTTUUV
VWWXYYZ

A B C D M N G P
E F G H Q R S T
J J K L U V W Y

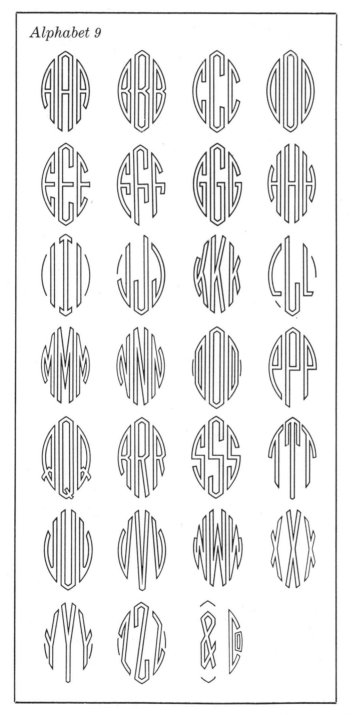

Alphabet 9

Oval monogram

Based on the oval monogram, this embroidered design uses two initials on the pocket of a man's shirt. The letters are set very close together, almost touching, and are worked with three strands of floss in a stem stitch.

Sometimes it is a problem to embroider on a pocket because you can't easily use a hoop. You must work with your hand inside the pocket while the other hand sews the stitches. To avoid puckering the material, don't pull the threads too tightly.

This is a good design for the corner of a handkerchief, the cuff of a shirt, a small purse or napkins. The shirt shown here is brown and white, and the monogram is done in wine color.

Freehand monogram

On a project like this shirtfront in which the
diamond shapes are irregular, use the shape as a
guide for the monogram. Distort the shape of the
monogram to fit the outline. The front panel is
quilted with white stitches. I went over each line
with a different pastel color to create a Mexican
look. The initials are satin-stitched in bright
turquoise. (See Alphabet 7, page 58.)

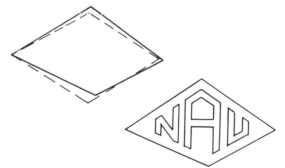

Back-to-back monogram

Add black initials to a plain white handkerchief. Some letters, like *I*, don't work to form a back-to-back design, but most look good. Trace the letter, turn the paper over and trace on the other side. Transfer each letter to a corner of your hankie. Embroider with two strands of floss in a satin stitch. (See Alphabet 16, page 93.)

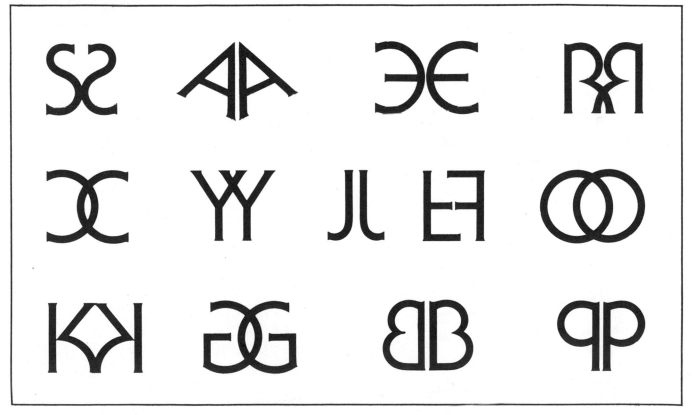

Linen napkin with border

A diamond square monogram is very popular, and if your initials fit into this design shape, you can create a neat and traditional-looking project (Alphabet 7, page 58). The linen napkin is white with a dark red border and initials.

Trace and transfer the border around the edge. Enlarge the letters if necessary, and transfer to the corner of the napkin where the border design meets.

Use a satin stitch for the monogram and a fairly large running stitch for the design. The little tassels are made of the floss and added to each corner of the napkin.

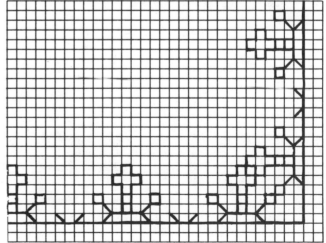

Tailored place mat

Make a set of simple tailored place mats from beige-colored Belgian linen. The classic monogram is perfect for many square items and is made up of three letters. (See the project on page 90 for another example of its use.) This monogram (Alphabet 10, page 67) is worked with three strands of dark brown floss in a satin stitch on the tight weave. You can execute the monogram with stitches that are less time-consuming, such as an outline or chain stitch.

Materials needed

1 yard of Belgian linen for four place mats; thread; scissors; pencil; tracing paper; embroidery floss; blunt needle; embroidery hoop; scissors; needle; seam binding; iron.

Directions

Measure and cut the material so you have four pieces 13½ × 17½ inches. Turn and press a ½ inch all around each piece. Finish the hem edges with seam binding that is either stitched or ironed to the fabric.

Using Alphabet 10, trace and transfer your monogram to the lower right-hand corner of each mat. If possible use a wooden embroidery hoop, as it creases fabric less, and a blunt embroidery needle. Remove the hoop when you put your work down. Linen will retain the crease made by the hoop more than most materials.

When the monogram is finished, pad your ironing board with a thick towel. Lay the place mat facedown on the towel, and cover it with a damp cloth. Steam press.

Variations

The square monogram will look good in many different techniques. You can use fabric paints to fill in each initial. You can cut a stencil and apply it to a recipe or file card box. Use this three-initial combination with cross-stitch on gingham, and cover the sides of a desk blotter.

Gift wrap ideas

Use your color combination for the gift wrapping. Beige paper with dark brown satin ribbon will go with this project. Insert a sprig of dried wheat under the ribbon, or tie cinnamon sticks to the bow. If you have a favorite recipe, roll it up in a scroll and tie to the package.

Monogram tablecloth

Even those of us who don't entertain often can find one special occasion to dress up a table. The circular monogram and border are done in pale blue on white. Before you buy the material, measure the length and width of your table, and add approximately 6 inches all around for the overhang.

Materials needed

Even-weave white Belgian linen; blue embroidery floss; embroidery hoop; tracing paper; pencil; scissors; needle.

Directions

Sew a ¼-inch hem around all edges of the linen. Press. Trace and transfer your initial (Alphabet 11, page 70). Use an embroidery hoop to hold the area taut while you work. Each time you put your project down, remove the hoop. Linen tends to retain the crease if the hoop is left too long.

Satin-stitch each corner with three strands of floss. Apply the design to one corner or all four corners, or enlarge it for the center of the tablecloth. The border is created with one line of cross-stitch. You will have to determine the size on the basis of the thread count. (See page 24.)

Alphabet 11

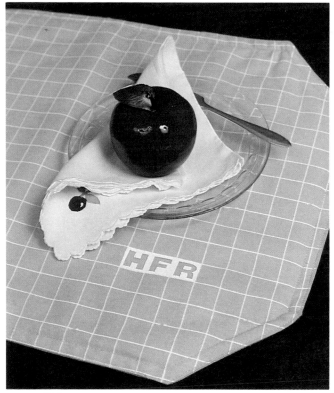

page 140

page 92

page 116

page 106

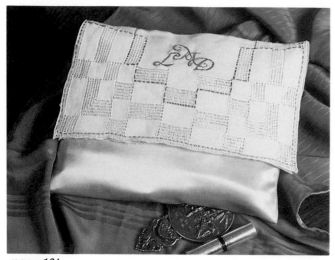

page 164

page 125

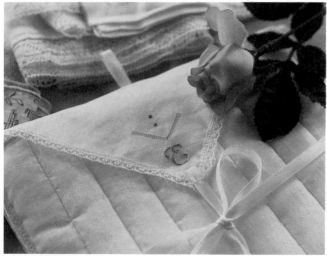

page 89

page 156

page 136

page 138

page 64

page 80

page 37

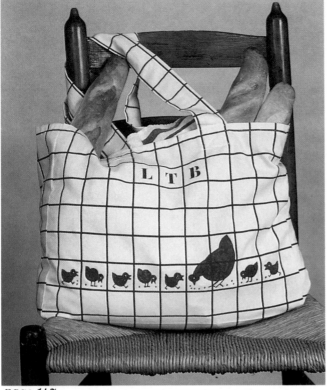

page 147

page 113

page 97

page 80

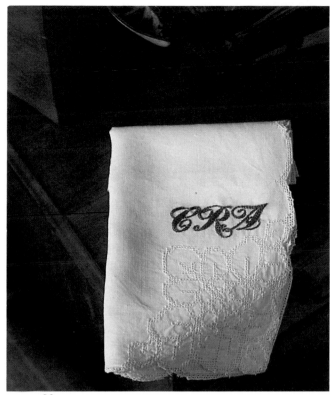

page 39

page 35

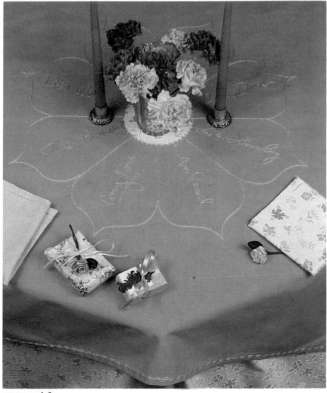

page 46

page 133

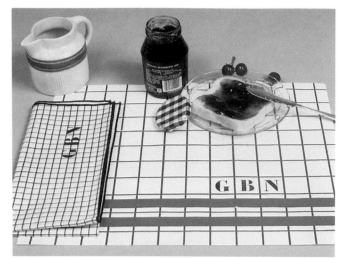

page 85

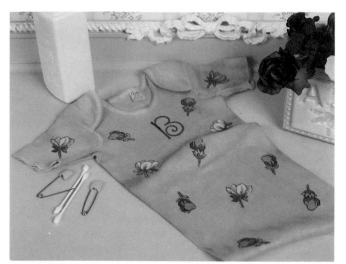

page 128

page 32

page 137

page 65

page 130

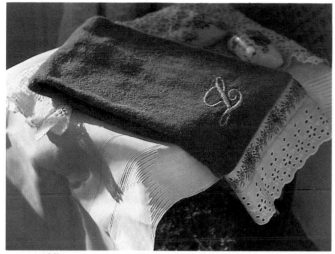

page 135

page 166

page 169

page 143

page 90

page 172

page 142

Fast crafts

Although most of the projects in the book were designed for quick and easy execution, some are especially fast and therefore serve as last-minute gift ideas. Time seems to be the one thing we all feel we don't have enough of. More women are working today than ever before and still bringing up families as well. Sometimes we yearn for a little more time to make the things we enjoy crafting for our homes and to offer as gifts. We know how much everyone likes a handmade gift. We like to set a table with something handmade. And we especially know how much money we can save by making rather than buying it. We also know how many unfinished projects we have sitting around the house or tucked away out of sight. It's frustrating because crafting is fun and it's satisfying to finish a project. So here are a group of projects that carry with them a guarantee that you will finish them in one evening—that is, one, maybe even two a night.

What makes them fast? There is little preparation involved, the materials are readily available, if not already in your home, you don't have to figure out complicated directions, the techniques are familiar, the designs have been worked out for the specific projects and each one can be completed in less than an hour or two.

Sometimes a craft project will involve a new technique that looks like a familiar, traditional one but will cut the time in half. Such a technique might be ball-point painting on fabric to look like embroidery. Though not as familiar as embroidery, it does not take much time to learn and to achieve professional-looking results. Sometimes the project calls for a traditional technique made easy. An example of this is the over-sized cross-stitch napkins on page 143.

Fast doesn't mean uninteresting or cliché design. Because the work is done quickly, each project has been designed to emphasize the personal aspect. Many of the items can be made more efficiently in quantity, thus are excellent bazaar, fair or fund-raising projects.

Tissue case

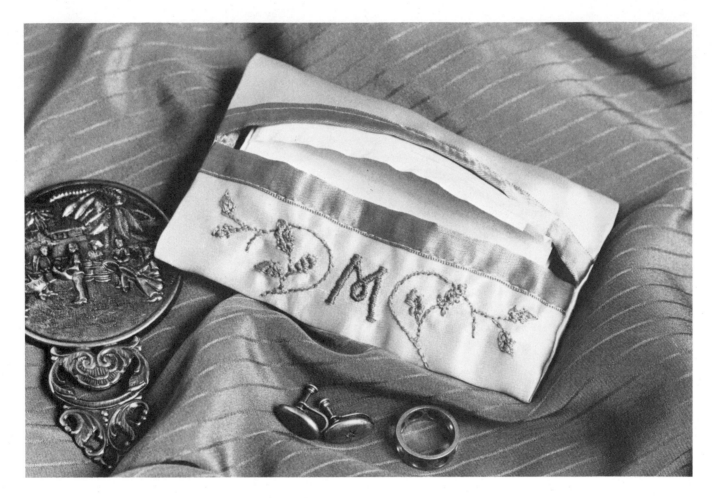

This small item takes so little fabric and time that it is perfect for a last-minute gift, stocking stuffer or spare-time project. Since the item isn't extraordinary, creative input is necessary to make it special. This is easily achieved by your choosing an elegant fabric and selecting a delicate design that fits the small space.

Materials needed

¼ yard of pink satin; 12 inches of 1-inch wide satin ribbon (purple used here); pink and purple embroidery floss; needle; thread; scissors; iron; tracing paper; pencil; small package of Kleenex.

Directions

Cut one piece of satin 6½ × 7 inches. Encase both 6½-inch edges in ribbon. With the right sides together, fold the ribbon edges in to meet in the center. Stitch up both raw sides, leaving a ⅝-inch seam. Trim the seams, and clip the corners.

Turn the case inside out, and press. A small traveling package of tissues will slip inside.

Embroidered initial

Transfer the design provided by tracing it from the book (Alphabet 12, page 76). Turn the tracing paper over, and retrace the same design so it is turned the other way. Be sure to leave room between the vines for the initial. Place the tracing over the letter, and trace it between the floral motif.

Retrace the entire design on the back of the paper, and place it in position on the tissue case. Rub over the paper with a pencil so that the design will be transferred to the satin. If the pencil line is too faint, retrace it on the satin with a soft pencil.

The vines and leaves are embroidered with three strands of pink floss. The initial is done in a satin stitch, using two strands of purple floss.

Variations

You can use velvet or taffeta for this project and make a decorative rather than solid ribbon border; because there is such a small area to be decorated, keep the design you choose delicate. If you use felt, cut out shapes such as leaves, and embroider only the letter. For a little Christmas item, make the case of white felt, and add green holly leaves with red felt berries. Slip a red hankie in with the tissues.

Gift wrap idea

Wrap the box with a delicate floral handkerchief in colors to match the case. Use the same ribbon to tie a bow.

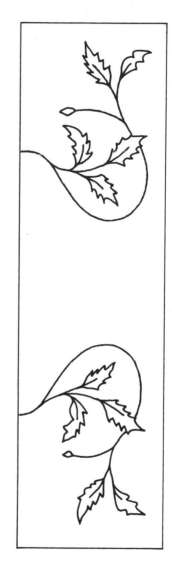

ABCDEFGHIJ
KLMNOPQRST
UVWXYZ
abcdefghijklmn
opqrstuvwxyz
1234567890

Lingerie case

Satin is a lovely soft material for a traveling case to hold lingerie and stockings. The inner pockets are made of a cotton ribbon print, and the embroidery picks up one of the colors from the print. Part of this material is used to pipe the outer edges of the bag. A delicate script alphabet has been chosen to complement the fine fabric (Alphabet 13, page 79).

These personal bags are becoming expensive boutique items, but you can make one easily and for a fraction of the cost. The finished case measures 9½ × 7 inches.

Materials needed

½ yard of satin (gray used here); ½ yard of cotton print for pockets; thread; wine embroidery floss; ribbon; clasp, button or loop; scissors.

Directions

Cut two pieces of the cotton print 13½ × 14 inches. Cut two pieces of the satin 10½ × 18 inches. Pin the right sides of the cotton fabric together, and stitch around the edges, leaving a ½-inch seam allowance and an opening to turn the fabric inside out. Trim the seams, and clip off each corner. Turn to the right side, and hand-stitch the opening.

To make pleats for each pocket, fold along the solid lines (see drawing), and press. Bring the folded lines over to the broken lines, and pin in place.

Pin this fabric to the front of one piece of satin so it is 4 inches from the top edge and 1 inch in from each side. There will be approximately 1 inch of satin left over on the bottom.

Sew the cotton to the satin, down the middle between the center pleats. Stitch down the side edges. Do not catch the pleats. Stitch across the center of the material as indicated by the broken line on the pattern.

Pin the right side of the remaining piece of satin to the pocket side of the other piece. In other words, the right sides of satin are now stitched together, leaving an opening to turn. Turn right side out, slip-stitch the opening and press.

Finish

Pin ribbon trim on the outside of the case, and fold it to the inside edge. Stitch by hand. Fold the bottom half up; then fold the remaining upper portion down. Finish with a decorative clasp, a button, loop or ribbon tie.

Embroidered initials

You have to be more careful when you transfer a design to satin than when you work with a sturdier fabric. The material is smooth and takes a pencil marking very well. Do not use the methods presented in the section on transferring patterns and designs. Most of the transfer pencils and pens bleed on satin.

Trace the initials from the book. Turn the

paper over, and retrace them on the back. Place the tracing on the satin, in this case 2½ inches from the right side and 1½ inches up from the bottom. Rub your pencil over the back of the tracing, and it will transfer lightly to the case. If you have trouble seeing the outline, go over it with a soft pencil.

Use three strands of embroidery floss and a satin stitch for the heavier lines and two strands with a running stitch for the thinner lines.

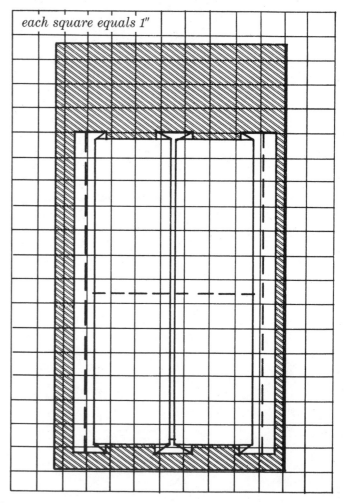

each square equals 1"

Quick gifts with needlepoint

Although it's always fun to make one more pillow or an illustration to hang on the wall, most of us look for quick projects now and then when we don't have much time for crafting. When you take the skills you've learned and combine them with good designs and new materials, it's very satisfying to turn out an item in one evening.

The needlepoint projects are all designed for plastic canvas, which is sold in sheets as well as in small squares and circles the size of a coaster. It needs no blocking, so it's ideal for bookmarks, book covers, place mats, boxes and similar items. These projects were done on 10-mesh canvas; that means 10 stitches to the inch.

Small skeins of 1-2-3 ply Persian-type 12½-yard pull skein yarn are used, making these projects inexpensive as well as quick.

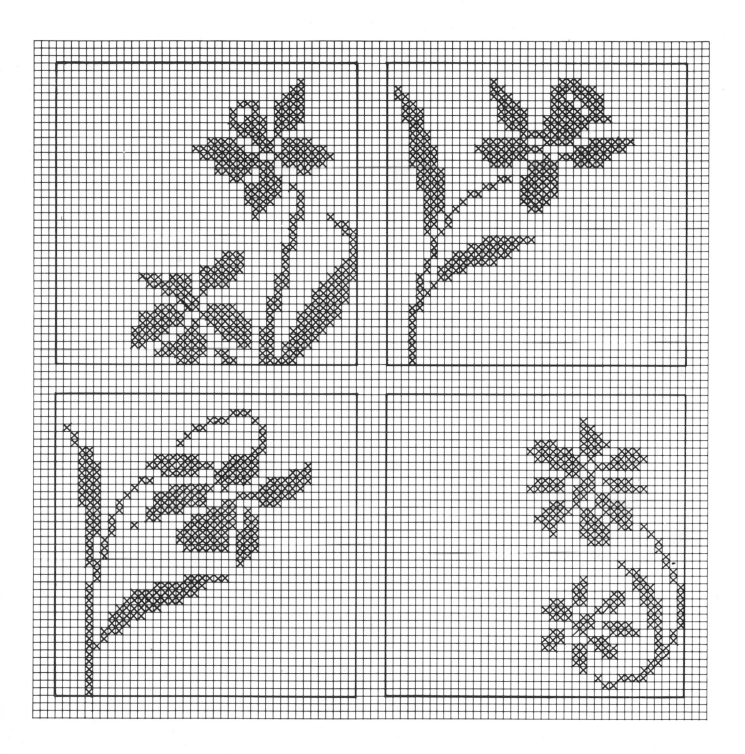

81

Materials needed

For four coasters and two bookmarks: 1 sheet plastic canvas. For the flower coaster: 1 skein deep purple, 2 skeins ivory, 1 skein medium purple, 1 skein green yarn. For the running border coaster: 1 skein dark blue, 1 skein light blue, 1 skein white yarn. For the bookmark: 1 skein deep magenta, 1 skein medium magenta, 1 skein pale pink yarn. Blunt-tip needle; felt or cork for backing on coasters (optional).

Directions

Follow the chart for a 10-mesh canvas. Use Alphabet 14, page 84, which is also charted for 10 stitches to the inch. All three projects are done with a continental stitch (see chart).

The background of the floral coaster is ivory. The letter, flower centers and binding are deep purple, and the flower petals are medium purple. The stem and leaf are green.

The running border coaster has a dark blue

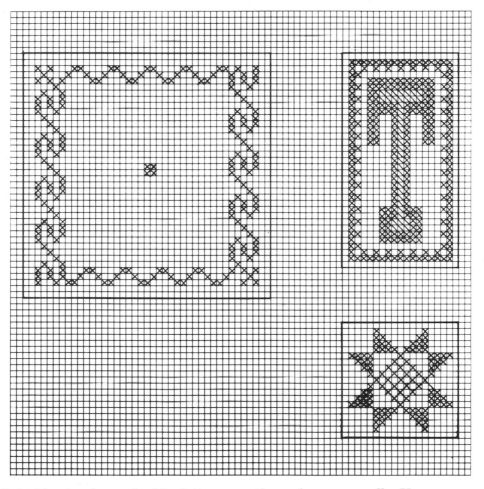

background, a light blue border and white letters with a light blue dash between.

The bookmark binding and outline of the letter are deep magenta, the running border and inside letter are medium magenta and the background is pale pink. The binding of the star and center design are deep magenta, the star points are medium magenta and the background is pink (see the color plates).

Variations

The stitches can be changed, and you can vary the colors as well. You can make a set of matching coasters, or do each one with the same design but different colors.

Gift wrap idea

Cut six pieces of plastic mesh, each slightly larger than your coasters. Make a box by hinging each piece together at the corners with a small piece of yarn. Put your needlepoint coasters in the mesh box, and tie closed with a ribbon. If the person does needlepoint, include a pattern and skeins of yarn with the gift.

Country kitchen place mats

Red-and-white-checked tablecloths, blue-banded pottery and simple white china reflect a country style. The scheme is cheerful and at home even in a contemporary house.

The vinyl place mat takes minutes to make. This fabric comes in different colors and is completely washable. No hemming is involved. You just cut the size you want and stencil the initials. This is probably the quickest project you can make, and the results are smashing.

Materials needed

1 yard of vinyl; metal straightedge or ruler; razor blade; stencil sheet; acrylic paint; stencil brush (makes four place mats).

Directions

Each place mat is 12½ × 16 inches. It is important that your cutting be absolutely accurate because if you are slightly off, the whole pattern will be lopsided.

Plan to cut between the checks rather than on the lines. It will be easier and look better. A metal straightedge or ruler is essential, and a razor blade gives you a sharper cut line than scissors.

Place the vinyl on a cutting surface. Hold the straightedge firmly on the vinyl, and draw the razor blade along its edge. When each mat has been cut out, lay it flat. Do not fold because the material will form a permanent crease.

The stencil letters used here are called Corbu and can be purchased in various sizes. Some art supply stores carry these individual metal stencils. You can use a stencil sheet from the five-and-ten, but you must be sure to select a size that will fit within the checks. Larger letters do not create the same effect. Alphabet 15 is provided for tracing and transferring.

Acrylic paint takes well to the vinyl and when dry is permanent. (See page 28 for stenciling how-tos.) Permanent waterproof markers can also be used for this project.

Variation

For added interest, make matching napkins. You can find checked material such as the fabric used for the shopping bag on page 146, or use dish towel fabric, contrasting blue and white linen or a solid bright red material. Use a variety of napkins with these place mats for a different setting each time you have breakfast.

Alphabet 15

AB
HI
OP
V
123

A case for delicates

This delicate lingerie or jewelry case is made from organdy and a lace handkerchief. It is embroidered with one strand of floss. You can purchase a similar item to embroider, or make this little case from a small piece of organdy and some cotton batting.

Materials needed

2 pieces of white organdy 7½ × 11½ inches; an organdy hankie or a piece of organdy 6 × 8 inches for the flap; 30 inches of ¼-inch-wide lace trim; needle; thread; scissors; pencil; ruler; tracing paper; pale pink embroidery floss; cotton batting 7 × 11 inches; 26 inches of ¼-inch-wide satin ribbon; pins.

Directions

Finish off all the edges of the 7½ × 11½-inch organdy pieces with a ¼-inch seam. Place the cotton batting between these two layers of organdy, and pin together.

Divide the material into 1-inch strips, and mark lines from one short end to the other. Quilt the body of the pouch by stitching along these lines from one end to the other. Sew lace trim around the long sides and one short end.

Measure and cut one triangle flap 5 × 5 × 7½ inches. Turn the edges ¼ inch, and trim with lace.

With the right sides together, sew the straight edge to the untrimmed end of the material. Fold the quilted fabric in half lengthwise so that both ends meet to form a pocket. Stitch the sides together on the inside edge of the lace.

Attach a 9-inch piece of ribbon to the point of the flap (on the outside). Attach the rest of the ribbon in the center of the back edge. Bring the ribbon down the back and up the front to tie.

Embroidered letter

Trace and transfer a script initial from Alphabet 8, page 60, which is light enough for this project (most of the other typefaces are too heavy for such light material). Use a soft pencil to transfer the initial. If the fabric is sheer enough to see through, you can trace right onto the material without the use of tracing paper.

Use a satin stitch for the widest areas and a backstitch where the lines are thinnest. The initial is done in pale pink, and two small French knots are added above for accent of color.

Variations

Although this project is made with the sheerest of cottons, you can vary the design by using almost any other material. Suede creates an entirely different look, yet it is soft enough to use for a jewelry pouch. This material can be stenciled with acrylic paint if you want to create a quick and easy monogram.

Gift wrap idea

Keep the wrapping delicate. Begin by inserting a lacy hankie or a sachet into the pouch; then wrap it with satin and lace ribbons and lots of tissue paper.

Versatile sewing bag

This ample 17 × 20-inch bag has many advantages. It holds all your sewing needs, whether they are balls of yarn, knitting needles, an embroidery hoop, half-finished needlepoint or even a pillow. The top opens wide so you don't have to struggle to get at your work. The rope handles make it easy to be carried as well as looped over a chair or doorknob. It's reversible. The monogram on the front is more than a decoration; it's a pocket for small items that get lost at the bottom of the bag. It can be made in an hour, and the cost is minimal, especially if you use remnants.

Materials needed

2 pieces of cotton fabric 18 × 42 inches (the pieces can be the same or different for contrast); small scrap piece of fabric for 4½-inch square pocket; needle; thread; 1 color embroidery floss; embroidery hoop; 28 inches nylon rope; scissors; tracing paper; pencil; iron.

Directions

Enlarge the pattern, and place it on the fold of the fabric. If the bag is to be reversible, the pattern is pinned on the fold of four layers of material. Cut and open both pieces. Pin the right sides together. Stitch around all but one narrow edge, leaving a ¼-inch seam. Turn to the right side, and press. Fold the raw edges in, and stitch. Fold the bag in half lengthwise, and stitch it up each side. You can use a blind stitch or allow the stitches to show as a decorative element. The embroidery floss will make the bag sturdy.

Create a channel for the rope by turning the narrow edges of the opening to form a 1-inch hem. Stitch to the inside of the front and back of bag. Cut the rope in half, and feed each piece through the opening. Sew the ends of each piece together, and pull it around so the stitched ends are inside the channel.

Pocket trim

Cut a 5 × 5-inch square, and finish each edge with a ¼-inch hem. Enlarge initials to be transferred to fabric. (See page 20.) The block letters are arranged so that the large initial of your last name is placed to the right of the square with the

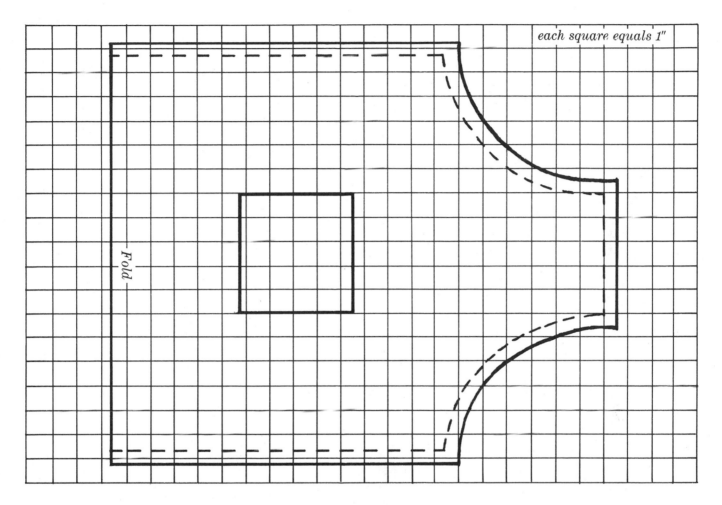

each square equals 1"

Fold

two other initials parallel at top and bottom (Alphabet 9, page 67). Use an embroidery hoop, and outline each letter with a back or running stitch.

Pin the pocket to the center of the bag, and stitch around three sides.

Variations

This fabric is blue calico with tiny pink, yellow and white flowers. The lining is blue and white, and the pocket picks up the pink with dark blue letters. The variations you can create depend on the fabric you use. Try to contrast the lining with the outside, and make the pocket stand out as a design element.

Gift wrap idea

Use several colors of yarn all together to wrap the package if it is to be a gift. For a knitter, stick knitting needles under the bows. For an embroiderer, wrap with bright embroidery floss and tie a pair of embroidery scissors and hoop to the package; a little package of needles and thread can be tucked into the pocket as well.

Say it with cherries

You can't overdo a good thing. Use a simple, cheerful design to create an exciting table. This is the lazy person's way to make quick and easy accessories. Find a fabric print that expresses your interest. Look for color and simplicity such as those in the overall cherry cotton used here. One cherry is applied as an appliqué to the corner of each napkin, and the initials are embroidered with colors to match.

This project was planned for a Christmas affair, but it can be used year round. Certainly the cherry tablecloth could enhance an outdoor table for a summer party. Imagine a large bowl filled with cherries for the centerpiece. Plain white china or bright red paper plates would look terrific. When you select your material, think about when and where you will use it best.

Materials needed

White cotton napkins; cotton fabric with a repeat pattern; fusible web (fabric shop); scissors; tracing paper; pencil; embroidery floss to match fabric; iron; masking tape.

Directions

Pin the fabric to fusible web, and cut out each design. Position the design on the corner of the napkin, and fuse it with a medium-hot iron.

If the cotton napkin is sheer enough to be seen through easily, place it in position over the letters in the book and trace them onto the material (Alphabet 16, page 93). If not, trace the initials on paper, tape that first to the back of the napkin, then to a windowpane and trace. If you are using an opaque material, see page 21 for transfer information.

Pick up the colors of the appliqué when you do the embroidery. In this case the initials are embroidered with three strands of green floss in a satin stitch, and a red dot is made, with a French knot as an added touch.

Variations

For a springtime motif cut out floral designs and apply a different flower to each napkin.

Gift wrap idea

Could you resist tying the package with a bunch of artificial cherries and some green leaves? If you use flowers as an appliqué, match the colors and find small flowers to tie on top.

Alphabet 16

ABCDEEFGHI
JKLMNOPQR
STUVWXYZ&

ABCDEEFGHI
JKLMNOPQR
STUVWXYZ&

93

Child's play

The projects created for this section are simple and quick to make. There are steps in each one that a child can do so that he or she can be involved in the crafting experience. Children like to see their names on anything. Even the simplest project here, the ribbon headband (page 109), will delight the child who wears it. It takes fifteen minutes to make.

Many of the projects are made from scraps of fabric, lace and ribbons and will cost almost nothing, yet look like expensive boutique items. For example, the baby bootees for a first Christmas stocking (page 53) could become a traditional gift for each addition to the family. The stenciled jumper is an example of a distinctive design that would be impossible to buy for the tiny cost of making it.

Aside from adding to the distinctiveness of a project, personalizing a child's item is practical. The design element identifies the child's apron at school or his or her boots left at a friend's house.

The alphabets used to personalize the children's items are childlike but in no way childish. They are designed to be used on a lot of things, and although some look like naïve handwriting, the letters are carefully planned to work together. These alphabets are legible and versatile. The precut stencil letters are also easy for children to read and have a unique style of youthful sophistication.

The techniques employed for the application of the designs are appropriate for children's projects. Some are simple embroidery; others are crayon transfer or stenciling.

The colors used for the projects are appealing to young children. Many are done in bright, crisp red and white; others are in soft pastels.

95

Reversible crib quilt

Nothing is more satisfying than making something for a newborn baby. And this project is fun, easy and quick. If you want to make it larger to fit a child's bed, simply add squares. This quilt is made of cotton. The squares are white and pink, and the border is light green. The embroidery is done in matching colors. The childlike block-letter alphabet is used for this project, and any letter fits within the floral design.

Materials needed

8 white 6-inch squares of cotton; green, pink and magenta embroidery floss; embroidery hoop; fine embroidery needle; scissors; tracing paper; pencil; 7 pink 6-inch squares of cotton; 1 piece of green fabric 36 × 42 inches for border; 1 piece of fabric 29 × 41 inches for lining; crib-size polyester batting.

Directions

Trace and transfer the floral design to each of the eight white squares (see page 21 for transfer information). Trace your initial (Alphabet 17, page 98), and transfer it to the center of each square.

Embroidery

Put each square in an embroidery hoop to be worked on. Work with thread about 30 inches long. Separate the six-strand floss into two three-strand thicknesses. Separate the three strands, then put back together before you thread the needle.

Use three kinds of stitches and a French knot. Satin stitch is used for the initial and leaves; the overlapping running stitch, for the stems; the lazy daisy, for the petals; the French knot, for the flower centers and buds.

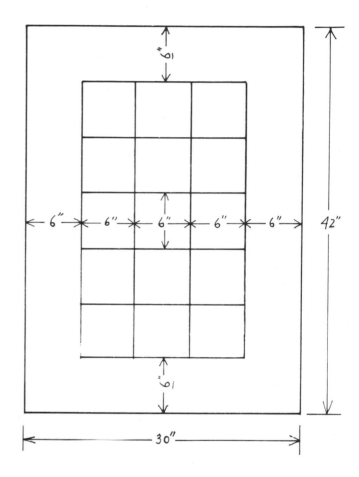

Do not pull the thread taut. Every few stitches twirl the needle between your fingers to keep the thread from twisting.

When the embroidery is finished, iron each square from the wrong side.

Putting quilt together

The quilt pieces can be sewn by hand or machine. You make five rows of three squares each, alternating the solid pink squares with the embroidered white squares. Pin the squares with the right sides together, and sew them with ¼-inch seams. Press the seams open.

When you have three strips of five squares each, place strip 1 and 2 with right sides together, and stitch with ¼-inch seams. Press the seams open. Repeat with strips 2 and 3. Cut the fabric into four strips, each 9 × 42 inches. Cut two of the strips down to 9 × 30 inches. Fold and press down 2½ inches along one long edge of each strip. Turn in ¼-inch seam allowance on this edge.

With the right sides together, stitch a long strip to each side of the pieced squares, leaving 9 inches at the top and bottom. The 2½-inch fold will be to the outside edge (not attached to the squares).

Next, pin the 9 × 30-inch strips, with the right sides together, to the top and bottom of the quilt, leaving 9 inches on each end. Stitch to the squares. Press all seams open.

To miter the fabric at each of the four corners, fold the fabric from the corner of the pieced squares to the outer corner where the border pieces meet. Stitch 8 inches along this line on the wrong side. Cut away excess fabric, leaving a ½-inch seam. Press open.

With the quilt right side down, place the polyester batting on top. Trim the batting to the exact size, 29 × 41 inches. Place the lining fabric on top of the batting. Pin the three layers so they will not slip out of place.

Turn the pressed fold over to the back of the lining to form a 2-inch border all around the back side of the quilt. Stitch by hand or machine.

Turn the quilt to the right side, and machine-stitch between each seam of every square through all layers. Stitch around the outside edge of the fifteen squares.

Alphabet 17

Variations

This project was designed to be made in a weekend. The embroidery design is deliberately uncomplicated for this reason. However, you might want to make a more elaborate quilt by adapting one of the other designs in the book. If you want to finish the quilt in a day, you could embroider one square in the middle and make a patchwork of colors for the other squares.

There are many variations you can try for this project, including the use of printed material with a solid square for the embroidered letters.

Gift wrap ideas

When you wrap this gift for a newborn baby, select a small rattle or teething ring to attach to the ribbon. Or tie a few plastic-head safety pins in a color that matches the quilt. If you sprinkle and rub a little talcum powder on the quilt, the present will have the faint sweet smell of baby.

101

Baby pillow

This little baby pillow is made to match the reversible crib quilt (page 97) and can be made of the leftover material in any size. The case was made to go over an existing pillow that is 9 × 12 inches. The directions given are for this size pillow, which you can easily make with polyfoam stuffing. If you use a pillow of another dimension, adjust the measurements.

Materials needed

2 strips of one-color fabric 13 × 4 inches; 2 strips of contrasting fabric 5 × 11 inches; 1 piece of white fabric 5 × 5 inches; a solid piece of material 13 × 11 inches for back; stuffing for a 9 × 12-inch pillow; needle; thread; tracing paper; pencil; scissors; 3 colors of embroidery floss; ⅛-inch-wide satin ribbon; fusible web (optional).

Directions

Trace and transfer the design to the white square (see page 21 for transfer information). The narrow ribbon border can be stitched around or attached with fusible web. Carry out the color scheme of the quilt in the embroidery design. In this case two shades of pink and two shades of green are used.

Turn one long edge of each fabric strip under ½ inch, and press. Pin each of the border strips to the white embroidered square. At each corner fold the fabric to create a diagonal line to the outer corner of the pillow. Stitch along this line on the wrong side. Cut away excess fabric, leaving a ½-inch seam. Press open. Blind-stitch the pinned border to the white square.

Pin the backing material to the front with the right sides together. Stitch around all outside edges, leaving an opening for turning. Turn pillow right side out and press. Stuff, and stitch opening.

Variation

If you want to make the pillowcase removable for washing, finish in the following way: Cut the back piece 2 inches longer than indicated. When you pin and sew the front and back together, leave an overlap of 2 inches so the pillow can be slipped in and out. Hem this opening.

Gift wrap ideas

You can give the pillow with the quilt or make it to be given alone. Wrap it in lots of pastel tissue, and add a tiny sachet or a bar of soap. Tie a small toy to the package ribbons, or use shoelaces with bells attached to the ends.

Boutique baby bibs

Baby bibs are easy and quick to make, and you can use remnants of fabric. However, because each takes so little—less than ¼ yard—why not go all out? Use beautiful designer fabric and embroider over the design, or use white piqué or soft cotton and create a darling illustration. We call this alphabet classroom lettering because it has a delightfully childlike quality.

Materials needed

¼ yard fabric; tracing paper; pencil; needle; thread; ½-inch-wide velvet or satin ribbon for ties; scissors; embroidery hoop; orange, blue, green embroidery floss; embroidery hoop.

Directions

Enlarge the pattern, pin it to a double layer of the fabric and cut out two pieces. With the right sides together, stitch around the edge, leaving a small area of the neck open. Turn inside out, and stitch opening. Sew a strip of ribbon to each side of the neck.

Enlarge the illustration, and transfer it to the bib (see page 21 on transfer techniques). Embroider on a hoop. The outline stitch is orange on the goose; the bonnet and butterfly are blue; the blades of grass and the name are green. It is all done with very tiny running stitches, except for the inside of the bonnet, which is filled in with a satin stitch.

Variations

A small blue floral print on broadcloth is an example of how a fabric can change an everyday item to something special.

I added a bright pink French knot to the center (Alphabet 5, page 52) of each flower. We call this alphabet naïve lettering for its simple freehand writing style. It was used on page 110 on the carpenter's apron.

Enlarge the child's name, and transfer it to the center of the bib approximately 2 inches from the bottom edge. Embroider it with a back or outline stitch in the color used for the flowers.

Gift wrap idea

If you can find tissue paper to match the embroidery, it will accent the present. Line a flat white handkerchief box with lots of tissue. Place a small item, such as a teething ring, in with the gift, and tie delicate ribbon roses to the outside package.

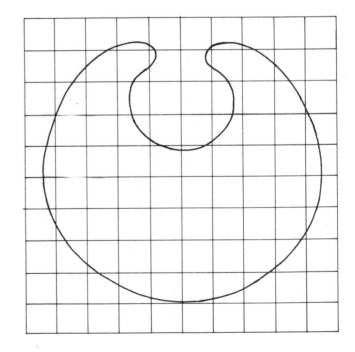

105

Preschool outfit

This is a basic dress pattern for a toddler size 2 sundress or jumper. It can be enlarged to accommodate a larger child. Measure from the center of your child's neckline to hemline for length; measure across the chest area to determine width. Enlarge this pattern, using the grid method to scale it up if necessary (see page 20).

This dress can be made in a variety of materials for just as many occasions. The dish towel fabric used here is sturdy and washable. The pattern creates a grid for a graphic design. The material is inexpensive, and the dress can be made from less than a yard. Make one for your own child as well as one to serve as a gift. It will take approximately one hour.

Materials needed

1 yard fabric; 2 buttons (the red ones used here are shaped like apples); stencil numbers and letters (art supply store) or use Alphabet 15, page 86; tracing paper; acrylic paint or ball-point paint tubes; needle; thread.

Directions

Enlarge the pattern on tracing paper, and place it on the fabric. When you cut the front and back pieces, be sure that checks meet at the sides. If you are using similar dish towel fabric, the border must be aligned as well.

Turn the bottom edge of the facing up ¼ inch, and press. Stitch close to edge, creating a hem. With the right sides together, pin the facing to the front of the dress. Stitch around the armhole, shoulder and neck edges, leaving a ½-inch seam. Trim and cut slightly into the curves, stopping short of the stitch line. Turn the facing to the inside of the dress front, and press. Stitch the back facing to the dress back in the same way.

Open the facings at the armhole edges and pin the right sides of the front and the back of the dress together. Stitch the side seams, including the facing sides. Press the seams. Tack the facing at each inside side seam.

Determine the length, and turn up the hem. Finish with seam binding, or turn the raw edge in ¼ inch and finish with a slip stitch.

Make buttonholes at each shoulder, and add decorative buttons. You might consider oversized buttons for added detail.

Fabric painting

Using the photograph as a placement guide, determine where each letter or number will go. Stencil each word and combination of numbers on tracing paper. Hold the tracing over the dress, and work out the best way to make a pattern. You may want to follow the design provided here or change it to suit your taste.

Hold the stencil over the fabric, and press down firmly with one hand while you fill in the area with the other. Ball-point paint tubes provide excellent results. Acrylic paint is also used on fabric and comes in a wide variety of colors (if you use this paint, you need a stiff-bristled stencil brush).

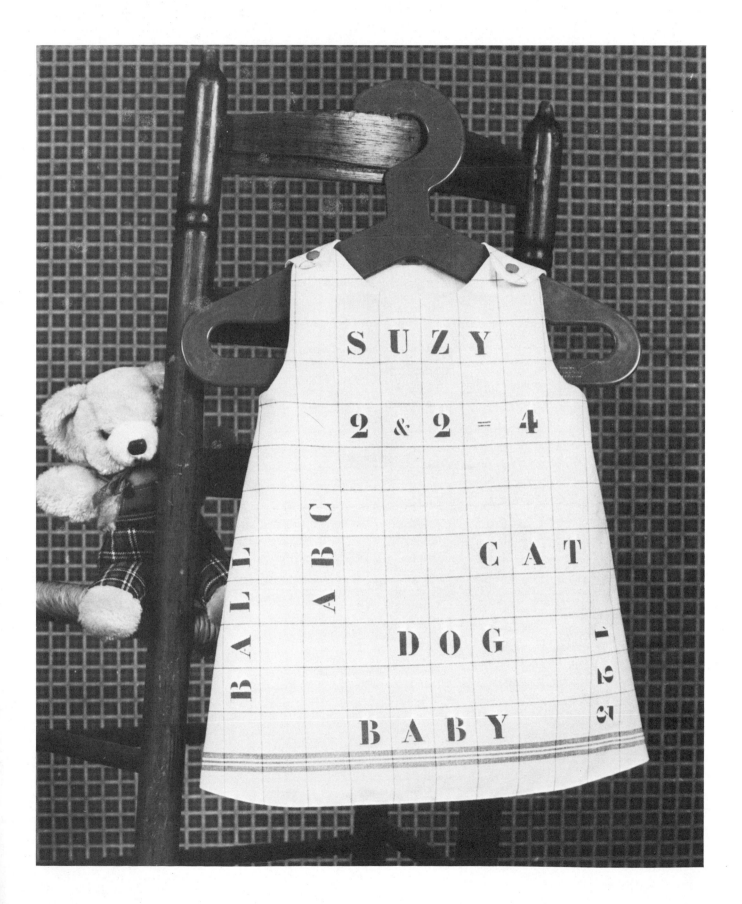

each square equals 1"

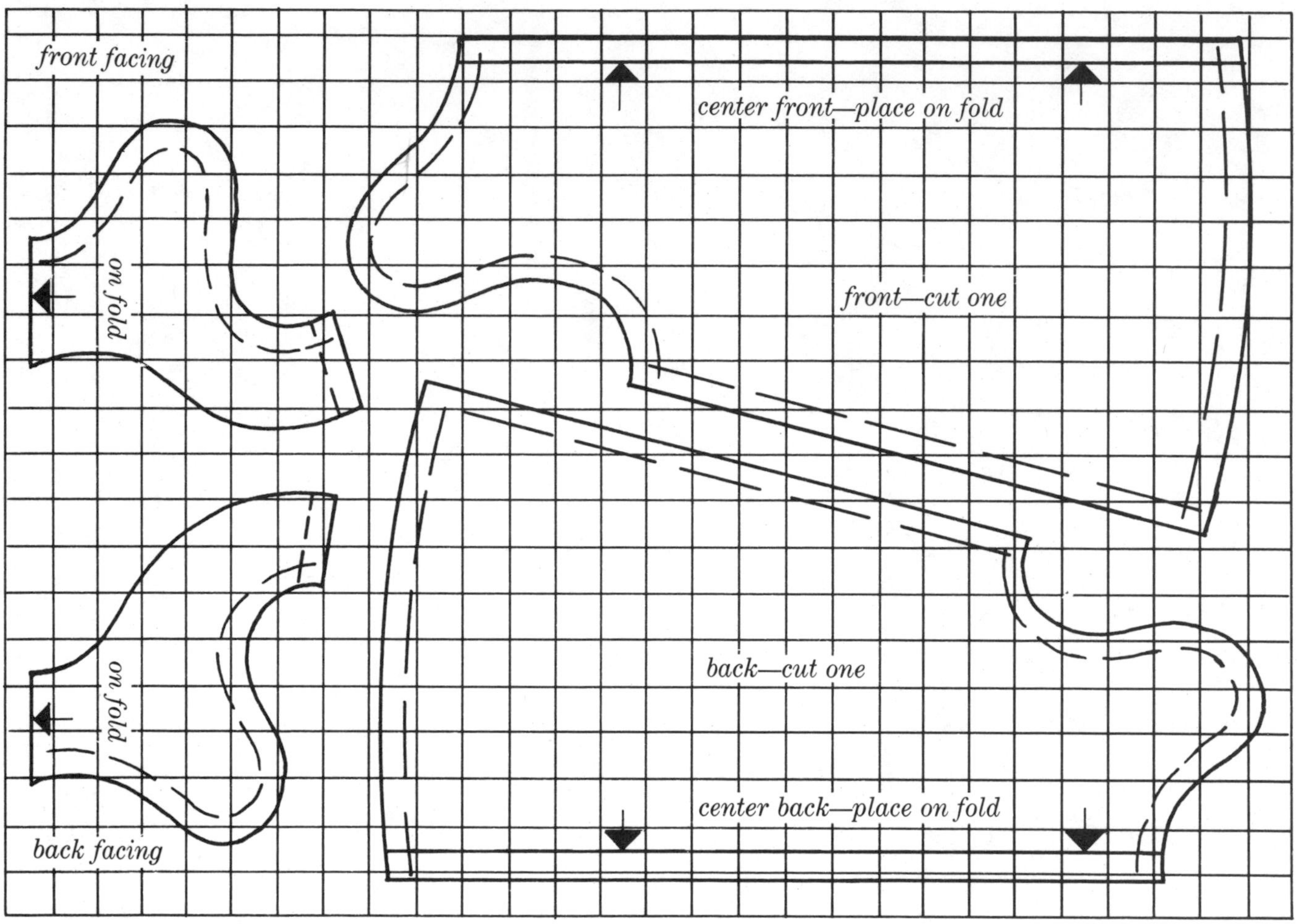

front facing

center front—place on fold

on fold

front—cut one

on fold

back—cut one

center back—place on fold

back facing

Variations

For a pretty party or holiday dress use red or green velvet material, and team it with a lacy blouse. Personalize it by machine-stitching a name around the neckline. Or add a large satin appliqué initial.

Gift wrap ideas

If you have made the red-and-white-checked dress, wrap the gift in a checked paper, and stencil the child's name and message on the package. If it is a holiday party dress, wrap it in dark green or bright red paper, tied with satin ribbons that have bells attached to the ends. Use the machine stitch to add a name to the paper (simply trace the name from the dress, and transfer it to the paper).

Beribboned

Looking for a quick last-minute gift? Is your child going to a party? This sweet little project is just the ticket.

All you need is 1-inch-wide grosgrain ribbon and a tube or two of ball-point fabric paint (available in art stores and five-and-dimes).

Plan to space the names with about 2 inches between in order to add little designs. You can write the name freehand or trace the naïve alphabet provided in this book (page 52) and transfer it to the ribbon.

Go over the pencil with the fabric paint tube. Make simple designs like rosebuds and leaves or a cluster of cherries between each name. Let the paint dry for a few minutes before you use the ribbon.

You can cut the ribbon to tie pigtails, or attach an elastic and button or snaps to each end to use as a headband.

Gift wrap idea

Consider making a ribbon to add to a present, and while you're at it, make extra ribbon length to tie the package. If the ribbon is to be the gift alone, make more than 1 yard, roll it up and put it in a clear plastic novelty box. You can even decorate the outside of the box with the ball-point paint tube.

109

A little carpenter's apron

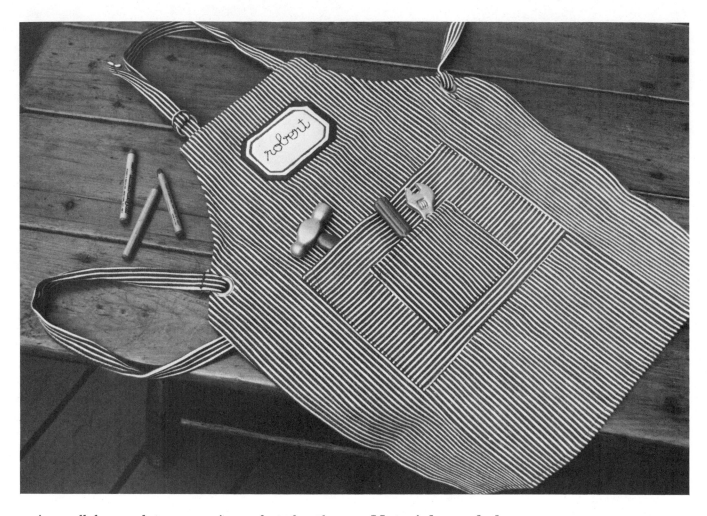

A small heavy-duty apron is perfect for the would-be carpenter in your home. It's made of brushed denim and can be cut, stitched and personalized in no time. The denim used here is navy blue and white ticking, and the apron is accented with red stitching. There is one large pocket for tools and a smaller one for pencil and pad. If carpentry isn't his or her specialty, the pockets can hold a coloring book and crayons or cookie cutters for baking.

Materials needed

½ yard of brushed denim fabric; red thread; black embroidery floss; red felt square; scrap of white cotton fabric (such as piqué or duck) for the name label; 2 grommets and setter (optional); scissors; brass rings for adjusting neck strap (optional).

Directions

Enlarge the pattern (see page 20). The finished apron is 19 × 15 inches. The large pocket is 6 × 8½ inches and the smaller pocket is 3½ × 4½ inches. When you cut the pockets out, leave ½ inch all around for turning edges in. Cut the body so there is enough fabric to make a 1-inch hem at the bottom and a ½-inch hem at the top of the bib. Cut three 18-inch strips 1½ inches wide for the neck strap and side ties.

Sewing

Turn the material in ¼ inch on the sides of the body and bib, and press all around. Turn in another ¼ inch, and press. Stitch on the machine. The red stitches are particularly attractive on the blue-and-white denim and add interesting detail. If you are using fabric other than blue denim, choose a contrasting color thread. The corners of the body are reinforced with a triangle of stitches.

Turn the hems at the top and bottom, and stitch them with double rows of red stitches. With the right sides to the outside, fold one of the 18-inch strips in half. Turn the raw edges to the inside, and stitch all three sides.

Attach this strip to one corner of the bib. Make a 1-inch tab for the other side of the bib. Slide the brass rings onto this, fold the tab in half lengthwise and attach it to the apron (see photo). The brass rings are available in craft and notions stores. If you don't want to bother with them, simply make the neck strap long enough to go over the child's head. Attach it by machine stitching to both sides of the apron bib. In this way the strap won't be adjustable.

Turn and stitch the other two strips, which will be used for the side ties. Insert grommets at each corner of the apron body (these can be purchased as a kit with the setter and are

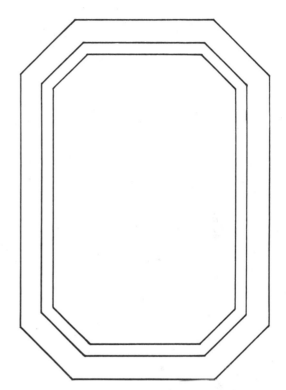

available in most notions stores). Loop each strap through the grommet holes, and double-stitch the fabric together. If you don't use grommets, simply stitch ties at either side of apron.

Pockets

Make a ¼-inch hem on both sides and the bottom of the small pocket square. Press. Make a ½-inch hem on the top of the pocket. Stitch across on the machine. Pin the sides and bottom of the pocket to the larger square, and sew them together. Reinforce each corner with a triangle of stitches.

Create a hem at the top of the larger pocket. Make a ¼-inch turn on the remaining three sides, and stitch to the front of the apron as shown.

each square equals 1"

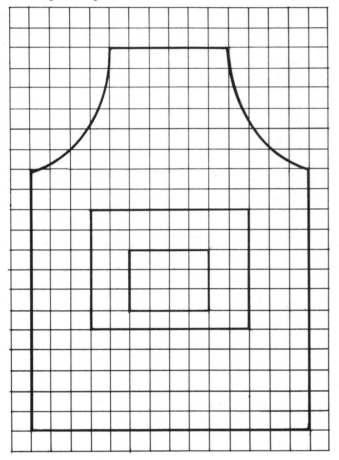

Label

The personalized label is created with fabric and felt and outlined with several rows of machine stitching.

Begin by transferring the name (Alphabet 5, page 52) to the white fabric (see page 21). Use three strands of black embroidery floss and a running stitch to hand-embroider the name.

Use the pattern to cut out the label shape, and turn the raw edges under. Press. Stitch the white label to the red felt, and cut out the larger shape.

Create the inner red band by machine- or hand-stitching several rows to make a ¼-inch width. Pin and stitch the label to the center of the bib just under the 1-inch hemline.

Variations

The material you choose should be sturdy and washable; however, there are many options for this project. The apron can be made from dish towel fabric (see the sundress on page 107), gingham, calico, broadcloth. The pockets might be made from a contrasting fabric. A red rickrack trim can be added to this denim apron.

Gift wrap idea

Wrap the box with graph paper (available in stationery stores), and tie it with a cloth measuring tape. Insert small tools under the bow.

Apron for a young artist

This simple child's apron is made from one piece of fabric and will take less than half a day to make. You might consider it as a birthday gift for a special child. If your child works with you, there is a step that he or she can do without help. Transfer crayons are used to decorate the edges and personalize the pocket. This technique provides a pastel watercolor effect. Tuck a box of crayons and a coloring book into the oversized pocket. The pattern provided here is for a finished apron that measures 18 × 44 inches and wraps around the entire body.

Materials needed

¾ yard of 45-inch-wide white cotton fabric, such as piqué; box of fabric crayons (available in five-and-dime); several sheets of white paper (such as typing paper); scissors; needle and thread; sheet of stencil letters (five-and-dime or art supply stores); iron; safety pin; pencil; pins.

Directions

Cut one piece of fabric 16 × 45 inches. Cut two long strips 2 × 45 inches and two strips 2 × 18 inches. Cut one strip 2 × 30 inches. If your fabric is only 36 inches wide, you can piece the strips. The seams won't affect the finished project. Cut the pocket according to the pattern.

Turn and press a ½-inch hem at each short end of the large piece of fabric. Finish off with hand or machine stitching.

Fabric coloring

The long strips of fabric are created in the following way: Rule off a piece of plain typing paper at 2-inch intervals. These strips will then be colored with the fabric crayons. The crayon colors will appear darker on the paper than when they are transferred to the fabric. When you

color along the strips of paper, change the color every inch or so; in other words, crayon approximately 1 inch of red followed by 1 inch of blue, then 1 inch of orange, etc. Each color runs into the next and doesn't have to be exact. Apply pressure to the crayon to make the colors dense rather than light.

When the page is filled with multicolored 2-inch-wide strips, cut them apart. Make enough colored paper strips to fit the length of all your fabric strips. Because the coloring needn't be precise, a child can help do some of it if you are working together.

each square equals 2"

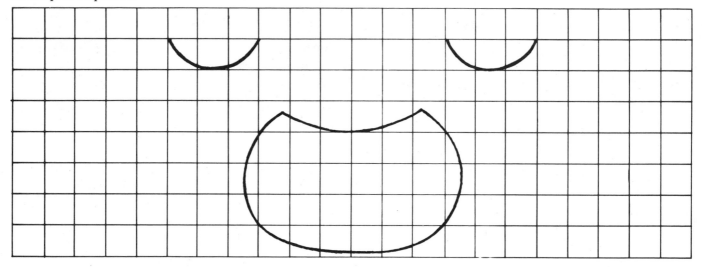

Transfer

Cover your ironing board with two or three layers of any plain, unprinted paper. Place a strip of fabric right side up on top of the paper. Set the iron for cotton. Start at one end of the fabric, and put a strip of crayoned paper over the fabric strip. Run the iron over the back of the paper, applying light pressure. Lift the iron and paper. The multicolored strip will be transferred to the fabric. Each crayon strip can be used once.

Continue to add color to the fabric strip in this way. If you run out of colored paper strips, either reapply the crayon and use again, or make new strips.

Once all the fabric strips are colored, fold all but the 2 × 30-inch strip in half lengthwise with the colors to the outside. Press. Turn the short ends in to finish off the raw edges. Press (sewing is not necessary).

Fold the remaining strip in half lengthwise with the right sides together. Press. Sew along the raw edges, leaving one short end open. Turn to the right side by attaching a safety pin to the closed end and feeding it through the fabric. Turn the raw edge in, and sew it closed.

Pocket

Draw the pocket shape to size on a piece of paper. Trace the stencil letters onto the paper. Hold the paper on a windowpane, and retrace it from the wrong side. Crayon each letter with a different color. The name will read backwards.

Place the pocket on the ironing board which has been covered with paper. Lay the crayoned drawing in position on the fabric. Transfer the drawing with the iron in the manner you used for the strips.

Turn the raw edges in ¼ inch, and press. Turn another ¼ inch all around, and finish the top edge with a blind or machine stitch. Set aside.

Apron

Open one long strip. With the right sides together, pin the edge of strip to the edge of the apron. Machine-stitch it. Turn and press. Turn up ¼-inch hem on the other edge of the strip, and press. Turn on the fold of the strip, and sew to the underside of the apron, creating a 1-inch band on the bottom of the apron. Stitch the ends closed. Repeat this on the top of the apron, but leave the ends open because this is the track through which the 2 × 30-inch strip will be fed.

Armholes

Cut the armholes where indicated on the pattern. The two 2 × 18-inch strips will be used to finish these edges. Open the colored fabric strips, and with the right sides together, pin them all around each armhole opening. The fabric should meet at the center of the underarms. Machine-stitch. Turn the other edge of the strip to the inside, and turn it under ¼ inch. Hand-stitch in place. Press. Blind-stitch the ends of each strip together for finished armholes.

Finish

Position the pocket between the armholes, approximately 2 inches above the bottom hem. Pin around the curve of the pocket, and blind-stitch it to the apron. Place a piece of paper over the pocket, and press. If there is any excess crayon color, it will come off on the paper. If you iron over the pocket without the protective paper, the color may bleed. Once it is set, the apron can be washed without fear of color fading.

Attach the safety pin to one end of remaining strip, and feed it through the neck channel. Gather material together as you do this, leaving a few inches of strip at each end for tying.

Variation

You can make the apron from one piece by adding an extra inch to the top and bottom of the main piece. Make a 1-inch border hem at the top and bottom, and transfer crayon on each strip. Place a strip of masking tape on the fabric to distinguish the area to be colored. Run cording through the bottom hem for a rolled effect.

Gift wrap ideas

When you transfer crayon to fabric, make a pastel piece of material to use as a gift wrap. Or wrap a box with pastel paper, and make ribbons from strips of the crayon transfer material. Tie a few crayons into the center of the bow. Use crayon to write a message on gift card enclosure.

Counted cross-stitch projects

Do you know a child whose name relates to a nursery rhyme, flower, color or famous person? There are many ways to illustrate a name. This charming picture of "Mary, Mary Quite Contrary" shows an example. However, you can add any name to this cross-stitch project.

Anyone can do cross-stitch, and the attraction is the perfection of the finished project. All the stitches are identical.

The design provided here is charted so that each square on the cloth represents a stitch. Once you get the first stitch in, it's very easy to follow the design on the chart.

Materials needed

Enough Aida cloth, 10 stitches to the inch, for a finished plaque 5½ × 6½ inches; red embroidery floss; blunt embroidery needle; embroidery hoop; masking tape; scissors.

Directions

Cut a piece of Aida cloth larger than the area to be worked. Tape the edges to keep them from unraveling.

Find the center of the fabric by folding it in half lengthwise and crosswise. Mark it with a pin. Count up to the top of the design to start. Remember, the chart isn't necessarily the size of the finished piece. Count stitches; do not measure to get exact size. (For how to cross-stitch, see page 24.)

It is important to use a blunt embroidery needle with the even-weave fabric. Use two strands of floss. Do not make knots under the fabric. Weave the ends of the thread under and over the stitches on the reverse side to secure them. Cut the ends short so they won't show through.

Variation

The birth announcement plaque can also be framed for hanging on a wall or door or be turned into a pillow for the crib or carriage. It measures 8 × 10 inches, the size of a standard frame. Paint frame to match the color of the embroidery, or you can make frames from illustration board that you pad and cover with fabric. This makes a nice baby gift or room decoration for your own child.

Gift wrap idea

If you can find small checked wrapping paper, it might be fun to write your message on the package in marker "cross-stitch" within the squares. Make the wrapping red and white like the projects.

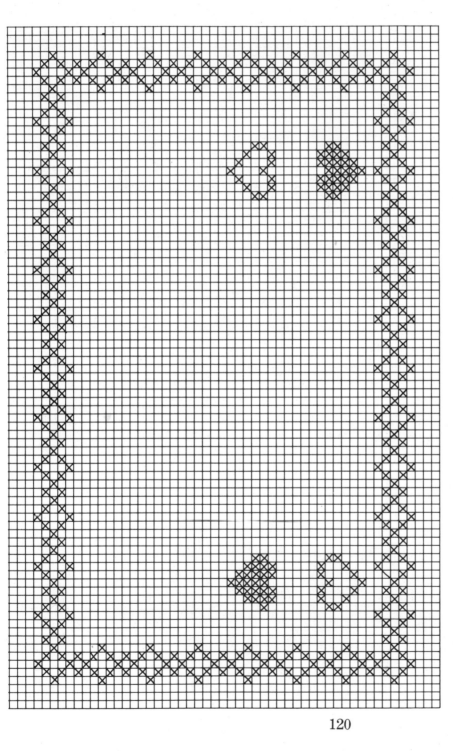

120

Ready-made to custom-made

Turn plain to fancy; add a decorative quality to a useful gift; make it better than store-bought. It doesn't take much effort or time to give a manufactured item a handmade quality by adding a name, initial or monogram.

When you shop for a gift, look for items that have this potential for conversion. Napkins and place mats with a grid pattern are perfect for a cross-stitch design; square items, for corner monograms.

It is especially satisfying to take a utilitarian item like rubber boots and make them decorative as well as more practical with the addition of a stenciled name.

Sometimes you can make something out of nothing by simply dying it another color, adding a little appliqué or embroidering a small initial. Don't be afraid to try some decorating ideas of your own. Often the item you buy dictates the type of design that would look best. Look at the ideas used in this book, but since your objects may be different, you'll have to judge for yourself which designs or alphabets will look best. This is part of your project's uniqueness. Everyone may be able to buy the same canvas shoes or handbag, but no one will have the exact ones you have.

Towels, aprons or totes might not seem like gift items, but they can be decorated and personalized so that these practical items have the special quality looked for in a gift.

Silk scarf

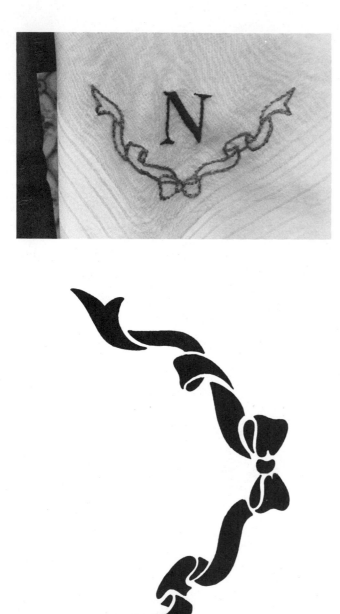

Add an initial and a distinct design to a silk or cotton scarf. Use the classic Roman capital letters of Alphabet 4, page 45, with the flowing ribbon and bow design.

Materials needed

Scarf; embroidery floss; embroidery hoop; sharp needle; scissors; tracing paper; pencil.

Directions

For ribbon and bow scarf: Since the material is so sheer, you can trace the design right through the scarf with a soft pencil. When you work on delicate fabric, use two strands of floss and don't pull too tightly. The initial is satin-stitched with dark green embroidery on the cream-colored scarf. The chain stitch on the ribbon is worked with medium brown.

For script initials: use a monotone effect by matching the embroidery floss to the exact color of a scarf. Since the thread and material are the same color, it is hard to see the stitches as you work. Therefore, trace the design on a piece of Stitch Witchery, which is a gauze-like transparent material, and baste it to the scarf. When you have finished embroidering, cut away the surrounding transfer material, and pull excess threads away with a tweezer if necessary (see page 24).

Variation

Embroider a scarf or handkerchief with white on white, and dye the finished project. This creates an interesting effect, and you have a wide range of colors to pick from.

Appliqué vest

Take a plain vest, and personalize it with appliqués and initial. If you make a vest, use a brushed denim or felt material. The appliqués are easily attached to this fabric with fusible web.

The appliqué designs are cut from polished cotton printed fabric. Choose any large designs that can be cut out. The small lacy floral stems and leaves fray when they are cut and should be avoided. Bed sheets are often a good source of designs for appliqué.

Materials needed

Vest; cotton printed fabric; fusible web; scissors; pins; tracing paper; pencil; black felt-tip waterproof marker; iron.

Directions

Cut out enough large flowers to arrange on the vest. Arrange the elements until you're satisfied. You may decide to cover the entire garment or to extend the floral border all around the hem. The design you have chosen may dictate the arrangement.

Determine where the letter will be placed. Trace your initial (Alphabet 19, page 126), and transfer it to the cotton fabric. Outline it with the black marker, and cut out.

Place each cutout appliqué on the fusible web. Trace around it, and cut out. With fusible web sandwiched between, pin design to the vest.

Set your iron at medium-hot, and start at one edge of the appliqué. Press toward the center. Work in from all outer edges. The appliqués will be secure enough to go through the wash, but it's a good idea to hang the vest for drying. When using large appliqués outline edges with zigzag machine stitch.

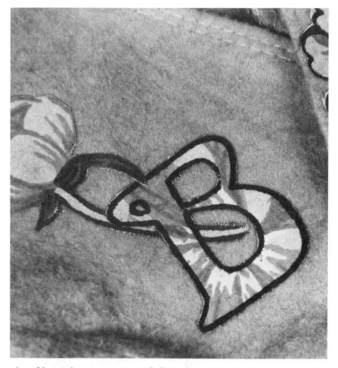

Appliqué is cut out and fused to rest.

Variations

This method of creating appliqué designs and monogram can be used on a variety of projects. Use one corresponding cutout for a matching skirt or handbag. Apply appliqués to director's chairs, curtains, etc. It's an easy way to coordinate a room decor as well as an outfit.

Gift wrap idea

Wrap the package with polished cotton fabric to which you have applied an iron-on appliqué. Tie the package with several ¼-inch-wide satin ribbons in the colors of the design. It will take minutes to create the wrap while you are making the project.

Boutique baby shirts

Carter's cotton-knit baby T-shirts take any color dye beautifully, and it requires only a few minutes to transform a plain white undershirt into a decorative outer shirt. If you can make several shirts at once, it will be economical and time-saving. Decorate the extra shirts to give as gifts.

Materials needed

1 package aqua Rit or Tintex dye; baby T-shirt; 1 yard of ⅛-inch-wide satin ribbon (peach color used here); printed or solid fabric (polished cotton or chintz) for appliqué; scrap of cotton to match ribbon color for heart; small piece of fusible web for appliqués; cotton ball or batting; fabric ballpoint paint tubes; pins; tracing paper; pencil; ¼ yard lace for ruffle; scissors; iron.

Directions

Dissolve dye in hot water per instructions on the box. For variety of color when you are making more than one shirt, leave each one soaking for different lengths of time; you will get lighter and darker shades of color. Hang the shirt to dry. Iron.

Find the center of the ribbon, and tie a bow. Pin it to the neckline of the shirt, hand-stitch around the edges and tack the center. Both streamers of the ribbon will be attached later.

Appliqué

An appliqué can be made from existing printed fabric, or you can make your own. Bed sheets are often used to cut out appliqué designs because the prints are versatile and you get a lot for the money.

However, if you use the bird provided here, enlarge and transfer it to a cotton fabric of your choice. Use a solid material, and paint details on

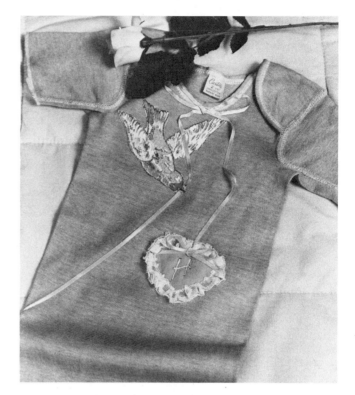

the bird with ball-point fabric paint tubes (see page 27), or choose a colorful print for the shape of the bird, adding an embroidered eye or detail on the wing.

Cut out the shape, and pin it to the fusible web. Cut the shape from the web. Position the bird on the shirt, and fuse all but the beak to the material by going over the appliqué with a medium-hot iron. (When the ribbon is attached, it will be secured in the bird's beak.)

Initialed heart

Trace the small heart, and use this as a pattern to cut two hearts from a scrap of cotton material.

127

In this case the peach-colored ribbon is coordinated with the same color heart. Satin or velvet can be used if desired. Transfer an initial (Alphabet 24, page 151) to the front center of one heart. (See page 21 for transfer directions.)

Place a small piece of cotton batting or a flattened cotton ball between the two hearts, and baste all around the edge.

Machine-stitch or hand-embroider the initial to create a quilted heart. Sew the lace ruffle around the edge to finish it off. Make a small bow from a piece of the ribbon, and attach it to the top center of the heart.

Finish

Cut a thin strip of fusible web for each ribbon streamer. Determine where each ribbon will end. The streamer that goes through the bird's beak can continue down the shirt and around to the back. The other should stop short where the heart will look best. Cut this ribbon an inch longer than planned so that the heart can be placed over it.

Set the fusible strip under each ribbon, and iron it to the shirt. Carefully place the piece of ribbon through the bird's beak so there is a piece of web under the beak and under the ribbon. Press. Continue to fuse the ribbon to the shirt.

Cut a small heart-shaped piece of web to attach the quilted heart over the end of the other ribbon streamer. Take a small stitch from the underside of the shirt to secure the heart.

If you want to finish off the edges around the bird, you can do so with a zigzag stitch on your machine.

Variations

This shirt is dyed light blue. The appliqués were cut from cotton chintz, but the flowers are provided here for making your own appliqués. Cut them from material carefully selected to match the T-shirt. Or cut them from solid polished cotton in a rose or yellow color. Cut matching pieces of fusible web, and pin each set over the front of the shirt. Be sure to leave adequate space at the top for a monogram. When the designs have been arranged, press the shirt with a medium-hot iron for permanent application.

Select an initial or two, and transfer (see page 21) to the T-shirt. Outline it with a fabric paint tube in a color that contrasts with the shirt, in this case, navy blue.

Gift wrap ideas

Because they are so easy and take so little fabric, make extra appliqués to apply to a plain fabric background. Arrange them in an overall design, and use this for the outer wrap.

Or use markers and the pattern provided here to make little hearts in an overall design on white paper. Transfer the child's initial to the center of each heart for a completely personal gift.

129

Informal napkins

A grid-patterned napkin is contemporary- and informal-looking. These napkins are inexpensive to buy, come in many colors and are oversized for buffet-style entertaining. This one is yellow and white, and the monogram is burnt orange.

This alphabet is called Helvetica, and the use of the lower case creates a casual modern setting. It is particularly good when used with contemporary dishes, place mats or tablecloth. The monogram utilizes the grid, and unlike traditional monograms with the last initial in the middle, each letter follows the next with the last-name initial at the end.

Materials needed

Purchase napkins or 20 × 20-inch fabric to make each napkin; 1-2-3 ply Persian-type yarn (such as Bernat); scissors; tracing paper; pencil.

Directions

If you make the napkins, turn and hem ½ inch around all edges. Enlarge your initials (page 20) so they fit within the squares on the material. Transfer them to each napkin so the initials are approximately 2 inches up from the bottom edge and 2 inches from the side hem. The placement of the monogram is another consideration for a modern approach.

130

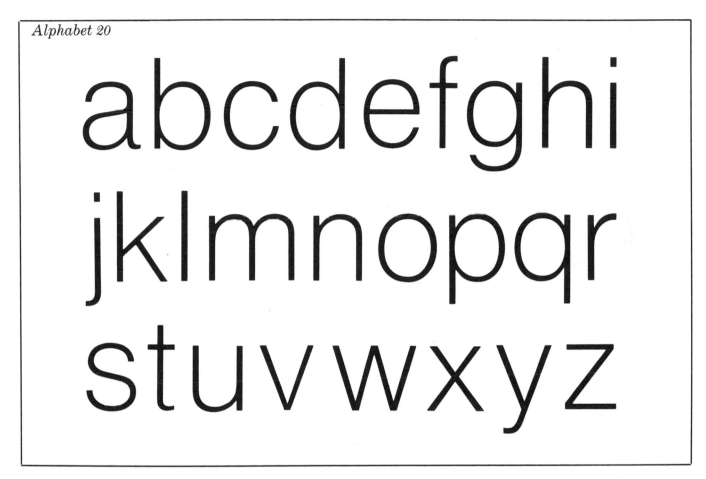

Alphabet 20

abcdefghi
jklmnopqr
stuvwxyz

Use three strands of the Persian yarn, and work each with a chain stitch.

Variations

You can enlarge the design for a bold approach and use dramatic color combinations for a different look. The yellow, orange and white combination is sunny and bright for a brunch or luncheon, but black and white can change the project for dinner settings.

This casual design is easy to apply to other projects and can be embroidered quickly. Use it as a stencil on note pad covers, a canvas bag or clothing. Use it to apply a name rather than initials on a child's sweater or blouse.

Gift wrap ideas

Make four or six napkins, gather each one in the middle and tie it with a ribbon to match the embroidery thread. Slip an iced teaspoon under each bow, and set the napkins into a box filled with colored tissue paper. Wrap the whole thing with white shelf paper onto which you've typed your favorite recipes. Stick a sprig of fresh mint under the bow.

A painted table runner

I like to collect doilies made of old lace, hand-embroidered tablecloths, linen napkins and table runners. Some of the work on these old-fashioned items is so exquisite that it's impossible to imagine the number of hours' work that must have been put into them. Often I come across something that is beautifully stitched but may be partially soiled or damaged, in which case I cut it apart to use for crafting projects. An item may lend itself to a modern design, or I can embroider new techniques with the traditional embroidery for an updated look.

The linen sideboard runner shown here has a wide cross-stitch border done in cream color on white. The floral design and script initial in bright red and green are added with fabric markers. Although it looks like a hand-painted design that only an artist can do, once it is transferred you simply fill in the colors. For best results and to ensure against bleeding, any fabric you use should first be treated with a fabric protector (such as Scotchgard).

Materials needed

Table runner (napkins, tablecloth or place mats); tracing paper; pencil; permanent markers (red, pink, purple, dark green, light green and black); fabric protector.

Directions

If necessary, enlarge the design, using the grid method (see page 20). If the fabric is white, you will probably be able to see through it to trace the design from the enlargement (Alphabet 21, page 134).

Spray a thin coating of Scotchgard over the material. This will retard soiling and keep the markers from bleeding. When you fill in the nar-

row stem areas and the initial, it may be easier to do a neat job if you use a magnifying glass. One that hangs from the neck will allow you to use both hands to hold and paint on the project.

Use the darker colors for shading, such as dark green for the veins of the leaves and red near the center of the petals. The very center of the flower is purple, and the outline of each petal and bud is a very fine black line.

Once the markers are dry, the color is permanent and the fabric can be washed without difficulty.

Variations

This design and technique can be applied to clothing such as a scarf, the back of a blouse or a skirt. It's easy to personalize with this method.

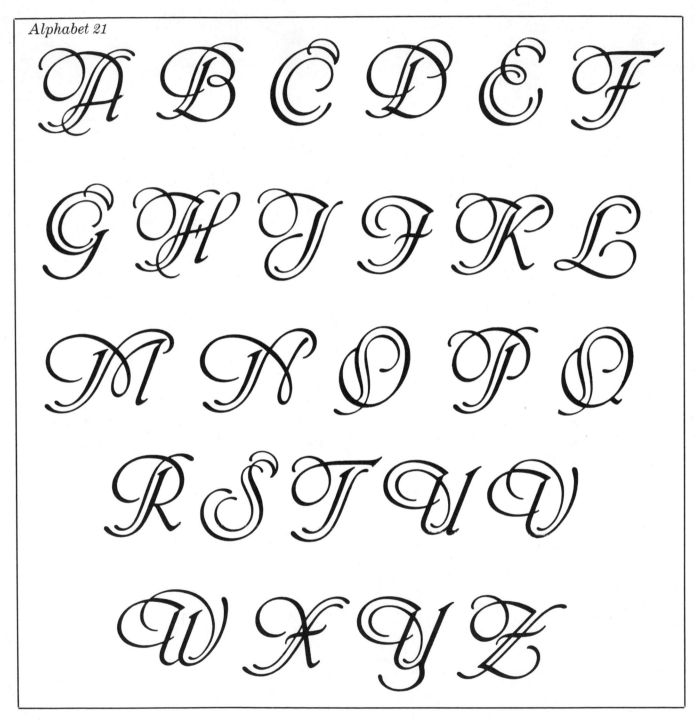

Decorator towels

Guest towels make a lovely gift for any occasion. If you buy plain ones in the color of your choice, you can trim them with lace, ribbons, eyelet and an embroidered monogram for a fraction of the cost of buying such an item. In addition, you'll have the opportunity to create a personalized item that is as simple or elaborate as you can imagine.

As I mentioned in the opening section, it is not easy to embroider on terry cloth. However, with a bit of care it can be done and may be well worth the effort. (See page 24.)

Materials needed

Good-quality guest towel; ½ yard of 1½-inch-wide decorative ribbon; ½ yard of 3-inch-wide eyelet ribbon; small piece of Stitch Witchery or organdy; embroidery floss; needle; pins; scissors; tracing paper; pencil.

Directions

Arrange the ribbon and eyelet on the lower portion of the towel, and pin them in place. Machine-stitch them to the towel. Leave the bottom part of the eyelet loose.

Enlarge and trace your initial (Alphabet 3, page 41) on the Stitch Witchery or sheer organdy. Pin to the towel approximately 1½ inches above the trim.

Embroider with a satin stitch, using three strands of floss for the thinner lines and six strands for the heavier areas. Stitch right through the Stitch Witchery and the towel. When you are finished, cut away all the excess Stitch Witchery, and pull out leftover strands with a tweezers if necessary.

An alternative method is to trace the initial on tissue paper. Pin the paper on the towel, making

sure that the letter is centered. Embroider right through the tissue paper. When you are finished, tear the paper away where it isn't stitched.

Variations

The variations for making this project are endless. Use a combination of contrasting ribbons, solid and printed. Trace and enlarge several different letter types to see which you like best. Consider making a matched set of three different size towels.

Gift wrap idea

Line a box with old lace, a piece of satin or delicate tissue paper. Insert a pretty bar of soap to create a sweet-smelling package. Tie a satin ribbon around the soap. Use some of the decorative ribbon to tie the box.

Canvas casuals

Canvas summer shoes lend themselves to many crafting techniques. Add decorative ribbons, embroidery, stencil, dye, fabric paint. These shoes are personalized with name tape ribbon, woven through white eyelet. Nothing could be simpler to do, and this added touch takes them out of the ordinary.

Materials needed

½ yard of ¾-inch-wide eyelet ribbon; ½ yard of printed name tape; needle; thread.

Directions

If you have name tapes left over from tagging clothes or from another project, now's the time to use them again. If none are at hand, they can be ordered from camping places and some clothing stores and through mail-order sources. Sometimes notions stores have initialed ribbon. You can choose your own design and have it made up with initials or your full name.

Weave the tape in and out of the eyelet, pin the trim to the top of the shoes and hand-stitch.

136

Everyday bag

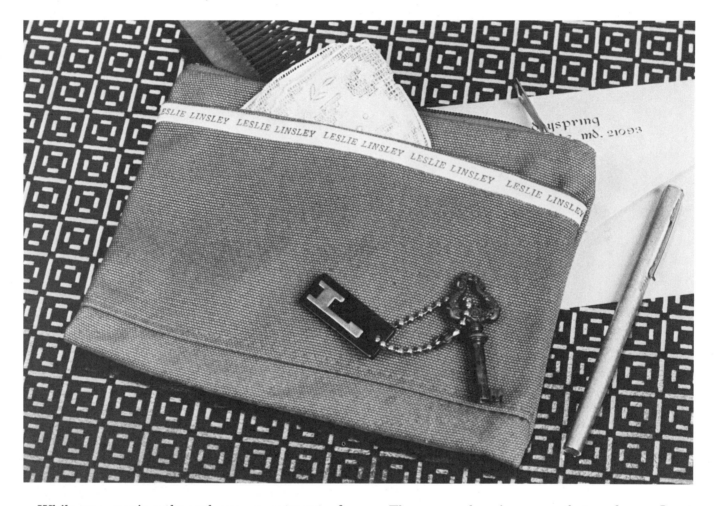

While rummaging through my assortment of collected scraps, I came upon several yards of iron-on name tape ribbon that repeated "Leslie Linsley" over and over. Obviously I am of the belief that almost everything will one day be put to good use if I wait long enough.

These name tapes have to be at least twenty years old. So here is another project to be personalized with the easiest method I can imagine. This time the tape is *not* identifying my camp T-shirts.

The canvas bag is a manufactured one. I cut the names apart, respaced them closer together and ironed a strip of my repeated name across the outside pocket. From a distance the blue-on-white letters look like a graphic design, and like a kid going off to school, I won't easily lose my belongings.

This idea can be duplicated on many items, which can be fun to design for yourself or to offer as a gift. Its one great feature is that it's quick.

137

Rainy-day gear

Rubber boots, slickers, rain hats are good items for stenciling. Your child will delight in finding his or her boots among everyone else's. You can use names or initials, large, small, placed up and down, across, down the side, back, over the foot, around the top, wherever you want. When you design these, do it with style, and use bright, bold colors consistent with the items.

Acrylic paint is wonderful for this project. If you make a mistake, you can wipe it off while it is wet, but once completely dry, it will not run or wash off in the wettest storm.

Materials needed

Stencil letters; acrylic paint (red for yellow boots, white for navy blue ones); stencil brush; tracing paper; pencil; boots.

Directions

Draw a guideline on the boot so your stencil design will be straight (see the stenciling information on page 28). Wait for each letter to dry before you go on to the next. This takes minutes.

Let the paint dry overnight before the boots are worn in the rain.

A touch of personality

The projects that follow reflect the quality of personality. Each one has been personalized with just a touch, turning an ordinary but often useful item into one of uniqueness. An example of this is the embroidered slip on page 145. The hemline had an embroidered cream-on-cream design. By adding a touch of green embroidery floss with a French knot stitch here and there as well as delicate script initials, we gave the item some personality.

Most of the things we personalize are intimate wearing apparel such as lingerie, a scarf, a handkerchief. The touch of a design should be appropriate for the object, and with most personal apparel this means using delicate and script initials or flowing lacy designs that complement the material.

Another way to add a touch of personality is to emphasize the person's hobby, style, color, interests or career. For example, the apron on page 149 can be just the thing for any wine fancier. This project integrates the name with the design representing the hobby. It is more than a personalized gift; it is customized.

Humor is never wasted on a project. A sampler with a favorite humorous saying, a pillow with a funny rhyme, a wall hanging with a cartoon drawing are examples of items that can be personalized with the addition of a name or initials.

If you have a favorite color, overdo it by using all the different shades in the project or emphasize it with white, such as the red-and-white-checked designs.

139

Contemporary place mat

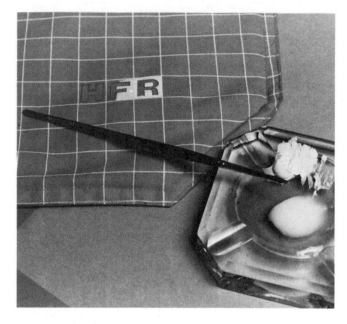

There are many contemporary fabrics printed with a grid or checks in different sizes. You can find place mats, napkins, aprons, potholders and other home accessories made from these fabrics. Take advantage of premade items to personalize. You have the opportunity to add your own creative touch. Whether you use the checked material for cross-stitch, embroidery or stenciling, the result is crisp- and fresh-looking.

Choose an alphabet that goes with this squared-up design. The straightforward block letters used here are scaled to fit perfectly within each square, and fabric paint is used to fill in the areas around them. If you are not using a premade item, this place mat is easy to make. It measures 14 × 18 inches, and the fabic squares are ¾ inch. The backing is solid.

Materials needed

1 piece of yellow-and-white-checked cotton 15 × 19 inches; 1 piece of solid-yellow cotton 15 × 19 inches; piece of polyester batting 15 × 19 inches; yellow thread; ruler; scissors; tracing paper; pencil; acrylic paint; artist's brush.

Directions

All stitching for the mat is done on the outside. If you want to contrast the thread for detail, use red or another color.

Pin the front and back pieces of the material together. Draw a diagonal line of 5 inches at every corner, and cut off this material to eliminate the corners. Unpin the fabric. Turn all edges of both pieces of material under ½ inch, and press.

Alphabet 22

ABCDEFG
HIJKLMNO
PQRSTUV
WXYZ

Trim the polyester batting to fit between the fabric, and pin all three layers together right sides out. Stitch around the edge of the place mat. Next, stitch another seam ½ inch in from the outer edge, making a double row of stitching all around. Press the place mat.

Monogram

Trace and transfer your initials (Alphabet 22, page 141) into the fabric squares. These initials are positioned 3 inches up from the bottom edge and 3 inches in from the edge.

Because the checks are yellow and the lines are white, the background is filled in with white paint. Use a pointed artist's brush and acrylic paint to paint carefully around each letter. You may find a magnifying glass helpful to keep you within the lines while you paint. Acrylic paint takes well to fabric, as do ball-point paint tubes. When the paint is dry, the material is washable and the paint will not wash out.

Variation

If you feel more comfortable with a needle and thread than you do with fabric paint, you can embroider the initials. The fabric square can be filled in with a satin stitch, or you can outline each letter.

Gift wrap idea

Make a set of four place mats and matching napkins, or make the napkins in a solid color. Wrap them in checkered paper, and either tie the package with a bunch of artificial cherries or insert two cinnamon sticks under the bow.

Lapnaps

Lapnaps are oversized napkins that are excellent for buffets when balancing food on our laps becomes a necessity. As with the project on page 143, they are made from grid-printed fabric. They are easy to make, or you can monogram existing napkins. The beauty of a grid design is that you can scale up the initials to any size and it will always look perfect. The lines are already marked for you.

Materials needed

Piece of grid fabric 30 × 30 inches; matching thread; Corbu stencils or precut stencil letters (available stationery, art or five-and-ten-cent store); acrylic paint; stencil brush; Scotchgard (if necessary).

Directions

Cut as many squares as needed. The finished lapnap should be approximately 29½ × 29½ inches. Either hem or finish the edges with thread, as shown here.

The stencil sheets come in different sizes; the one used for this project is for 1½-inch-high letters. Because the checked material is navy and white, the paint is cherry red for a bright contrast. Position the stencil so it falls right on the line. Hold the material firmly while you apply the paint.

To stencil initials

If you use acrylic paint, squeeze a little bit into a dish. Tap the brush on the paint, and then tap it several times on a piece of paper. For stenciling, the brush should be almost dry. It is better to go over and over the area to be filled in than to apply a lot of paint at once. (See the tips on stenciling, page 28.)

Variations

Another version of the project is shown with embroidered initials on page 131.

Gift wrap idea

Inasmuch as these lapnaps are intended for buffets, it might be nice to tie a bunch of napkin rings to the package. You can get plain wooden rings and paint them with the acrylic to match the monogram.

Cross-stitch napkins

There are many ready-made napkins with large, small or medium-sized checks. For a quick touch of the personal or for an instant holiday accessory, create your initials in cross-stitch. For this project I used six strands of red embroidery floss on a black-and-white grid napkin. Each cross-stitch fills the square so that the letters are big and bold. The size of your letters will be determined by the size of the napkin and the squares to be filled. Oversized napkins with very large letters will give you a dramatic setting whether you lay them out together for a buffet or place one at each setting.

The materials needed for this project are few, and it could easily be listed under the fast craft section because it will take you less than twenty minutes to complete. But this design gives an otherwise plain napkin some pizzazz.

Materials needed

Napkins; embroidery hoop; blunt needle; cotton floss; scissors.

Directions

Refer to cross-stitch information on page 24 for helpful hints.

To keep the stitches looking neat, separate each of the six strands of floss; then put them together to thread the needle. The embroidery hoop is essential for holding the fabric taut because you are working within a large area and taking large stitches. Do not make any knots under the fabric; when each letter is complete, end the thread by weaving under a few stitches. Cut the end fairly close to the material, and begin the next letter. In this way you won't be taking the thread across a large area of fabric which may show through to the front.

Variations

There are many examples in the book of other designs from this kind of fabric pattern. Look at them to see how many different ways you can make the same napkin.

Gift wrap idea

Use solid-color paper, and rule off the person's initials with a cross-stitch design in colored marker. Or if you can find grid paper to match the napkins, you can use it plain or add the *X*'s, as suggested above.

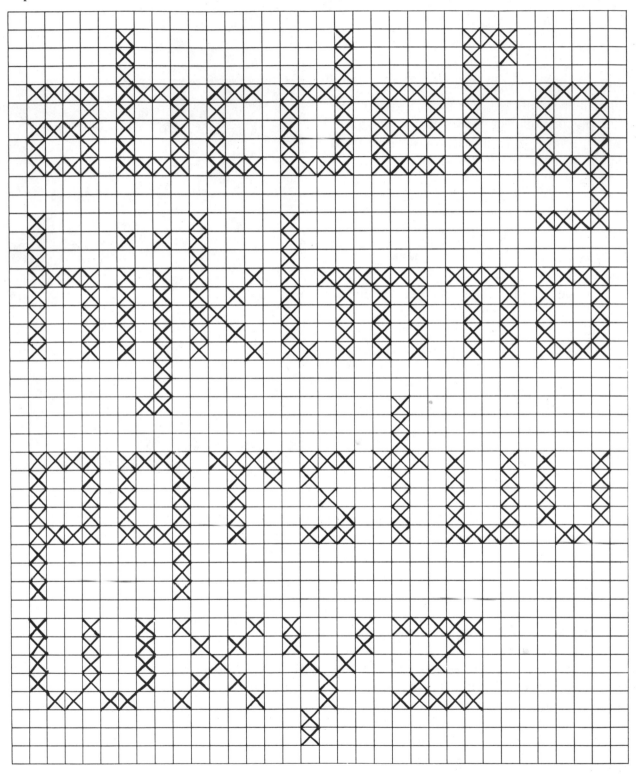

Slip into something personal

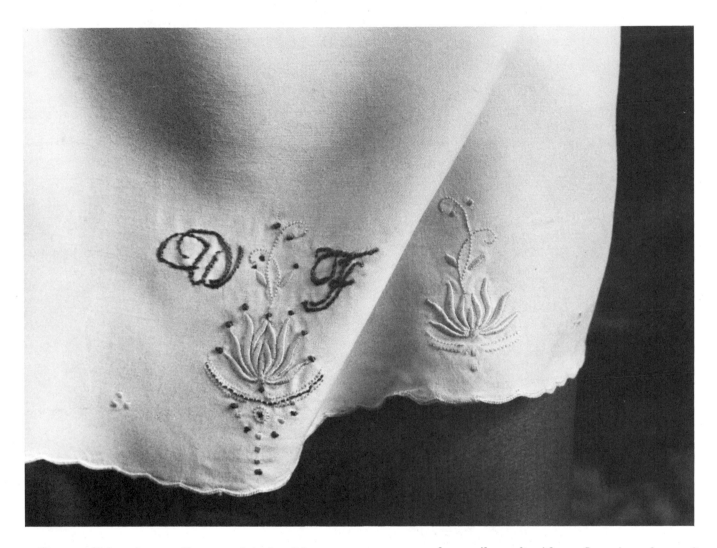

Personalizing is usually associated with personal items. It might be a lacy hankie with an embroidered initial, a lingerie case, a nightgown, a bathrobe or a slip. Often such garments are machine-embroidered, and this is the perfect area for a creative touch.

Add color to the existing design. Embellish the design to be more elaborate. Work your initials into the design. All you need is tracing paper and pencil, embroidery floss in colors of your choice and a needle. When the fabric of the slip is silk, silk thread is best. However, it is often difficult to find and not as easy to work with as cotton floss.

Use Alphabet 21, page 134, for this project unless there is another script that works better with your item. (See the transfer information on page 21 and embroidery stitches on page 25.)

145

146

Country tote

This soft shopping bag can be made for a variety of purposes. I like it as a marketing bag, but it is just as useful for taking towels and lunch to the beach. It can be used as a school bag or for carrying sewing projects.

The bright and cheerful fabric is red-and-white-checked, and the initials and chickens are applied with ball-point fabric tubes.

The overall size is 15½ × 12 × 4 inches deep. The handles are 12 inches long to fit over the shoulder, but you can adjust them for your use.

Materials needed

1 yard of sturdy cotton fabric; scissors; thread; stencil letters; tracing paper; pencil; permanent marker or ball-point fabric paint tube; pins.

Directions

The front, bottom and back are made from one piece of fabric; cut this piece 29 × 16 inches. Cut two pieces for the sides 5 × 13 inches. Cut two strips 3 × 25 inches for the handles.

Pin the side panels to the front and back and bottom section. Because there is no separate bottom piece, measure down 12½ inches from the top edge of the front, and iron a crease. Do the same on the back. You will now have a clearly delineated 4-inch bottom panel. With the right sides together, sew the side panels to the front and back of the bag and across the bottom. Turn right side out.

Turn the top edge down to form a ½-inch hem. Press and stitch. Next, create the handles by folding the material in half lengthwise so that the checks line up with those on the bag. In this case, the material is folded to the underside of the strap so that it overlaps. Stitch.

Pin the straps to front and back of the bag 4

inches in from the side seam, with approximately 4 inches between them. Reinforce with an *X* stitching where the handle attaches to the bag.

Adding the design

Place newspaper inside the bag under the area to be stenciled. Position each stencil letter in the center of one of the checks. They should be in the center of the bag approximately 2 inches from the top depending on the fabric you are using.

Trace and transfer the chickens and the hen to the bottom portion of your bag. Be sure the newspaper is under the area to be painted. Fill in all but the eyes with the fabric paint. Make dots for chicken feed. Let it dry before using.

Variation

If the bag is to be used as a beach tote, you can easily line it with waterproof material. Cut all pieces, except those used for the handles, exactly the same. Any fabric can be used for this project as long as the solid color used for the design contrasts enough to show up.

Gift wrap idea

Use checkered paper for wrapping, and color a few chickens walking across the box. It's easy to do, takes minutes and is an inexpensive way to create customized wrapping paper.

Wine taster's apron

For barbecues, bartending or just plain everyday cooking, make him a large wine taster's apron. This one is bright red, and just for fun the French version of his name is used. Acrylic paint and a wine cork are the bases for the stenciled design. Two large pockets on the front hold everything one could need.

Materials needed

1 yard of red cotton duck; white and dark green acrylic paint; No. 3 tapered paintbrush; wine cork; stencil brush; waxed stencil paper; tracing paper; pencil; X-Acto or craft knife; tape; scissors; red thread; pins; masking tape.

Directions

Enlarge the pattern so that the finished apron will measure 34 inches long, 30 inches across the body and 11 inches across the bib. Place the pattern on the fold of the fabric, and cut the double layer. Open the material, and hem around all edges. There is a 1-inch hem on the top edge and a ¼-inch hem on all other edges.

Cut a piece of material 9½ × 18½ inches for the pockets. Turn and stitch a ¼-inch hem at the top and bottom. Turn the side edges in ¼ inch, and press. Pin the sides of the pocket to the center of the apron approximately 13 inches from the top. Find the center, and draw a line from the top edge to the bottom of the pocket.

Stitch the pocket to the apron, and stitch down the center line to divide the pocket in two. Cut two strips of material 23 × 1½ inches and two strips 20 × 1½ inches for the side and neck ties.

Turn all the edges in, fold the material lengthwise and stitch close to the edge. Attach the longest strips to both sides of the apron. Attach the shorter strips to both sides of the bib.

Stenciling design

Enlarge the name (Alphabet 24, page 151) and transfer it by rubbing the pencil lines onto the apron. Paint each letter with the paintbrush and white acrylic paint.

Enlarge the leaf design on tracing paper. Tape the tracing paper to the waxed stencil paper, and cut the stencil with an X-Acto or craft knife. Tape the stencil in position over the top of the apron pocket. Using the stencil brush, tap the dark green paint over the cutaway areas (see page 28).

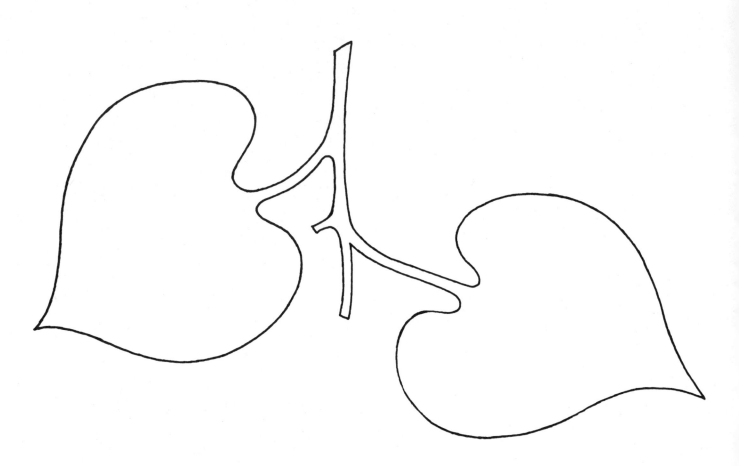

To create the bunch of grapes, begin by mixing white paint with the green paint so that it produces a light green. Using the cork from a wine bottle, stencil the grapes at random until you have a bunch. Perfection is not necessary here. Just keep adding grapes until the design seems full enough. The photo will help. Do all the grapes once over lightly. When they are dry, go over some of them to whiten. When the paint is dry, the design is permanent and the apron is washable.

Variation

Another version might be a white apron with red cherries on the pocket. Use the same technique. You can even use the leaves and stem and create cherries at the ends of the stem.

Gift wrap idea

This gift practically demands to be given with a bottle of wine. If you can collect enough labels, use them to cover the box in which you wrap the apron. If you can't put enough labels together, use deep purple paper and stencil white grapes on top.

No-cost, low-cost gifts

Aside from well-designed, personalized, easy to make, is there any quality more appreciated in a craft project than no or low cost? The following projects are made from leftovers, scraps, throwaways, small bits of material, ribbons, a button, a piece of lace. However, just because it's made from scraps doesn't mean it has to look like a throwaway item. These projects utilized everyday materials and are as carefully designed as the rest of the projects. Ingenuity can often replace time and expense.

The little sewing kits and the eyeglass case are examples of how interesting ribbons, pretty printed lining material or a piece of velvet can turn out big results. True, velvet or satin is usually expensive, but when you use so little, you can afford to be extravagant.

I save old doilies, lace and coasters, which I often combine with ribbon and embroidery to make lingerie cases, an evening bag, a sachet. If you have a worn tablecloth, consider cutting it up to make some of these projects.

Throwaway items such as cookie tins, butter tubs, and jars can be used as the basic element for a project. Such is the case with the sewing box on page 169, which is a cookie tin covered with designer fabric left over from another project. A bid of padding, lace and embroidering floss are the other ingredients. Look at that tissue tube, detergent box, mushroom basket before you toss them out. There's potential in yesterday's garbage.

Eyeglass case

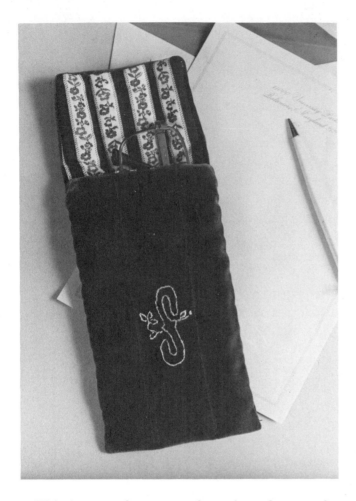

This is a good scrap craft project that can be made with under ¼ yard of fabric. The embroidered design and letter are deliberately simple because the fabric is velvet, which is difficult to work on. However, its softness is good for this project.

Materials Needed

¼ yard of velvet fabric; ¼ yard of cotton lining; blue and pink embroidery floss; needle; dressmaker's carbon or transfer pen; tracing paper; thread; scissors; small snap for closing.

Directions

Cut a piece of velvet and a piece of cotton for the lining 17 × 4½ inches. Pin the right sides together, and stitch around three sides, leaving an opening on one short end for turning. Turn to the right side, and blind-stitch the opening.

Divide the material equally into three sections, and machine-stitch the length of the fabric to create quilting.

Turn the fabric up 7 inches with the velvet to the outside. This will form the pocket for the glasses. Slip-stitch the sides. Sew a snap to the inside center, and turn the top flap down.

Applying design

It is difficult to transfer a design to velvet, especially if it is dark. Use dressmaker's carbon or a transfer pen. If necessary, go over the design with a marker.

The blue letter (Alphabet 25, page 155) is outlined with a backstitch, but you may choose to fill it in. The pink flowers are incorporated into the initial and can be made more elaborate if you want to put more work into the project.

Variations

The surprise in this case is the lining. Select fabric that contrasts. You can be as imaginative as you like. Often the material, color or pattern dictates who will use the item. For example, denim might be used for a teenager's sunglass case; line the inside with waterproof material. Or make a case of suede, and line it with wool or corduroy. Suede takes acrylic paint well; try a stenciled initial.

A black velvet evening case can be lined with red satin. And a lace handkerchief can be padded and used to make a very dainty eyeglass case.

Classic collars

Make a collar for yourself and one for a friend, or dress up a sweater for your favorite child. They are a cinch to make and can be decorated with a variety of techniques as well as trimmings. Use a bit of lace for one, rickrack for another and piping for a third. Each pattern is slightly different in design but is made from one piece of fabric.

Materials needed

½ yard of cotton fabric, such as piqué; embroidery floss; needle; fabric crayons or paint (optional); lace or eyelet trim.

Directions

Enlarge the pattern of your choice, and place on the fold of the fabric. Cut two pieces of the pattern. Unfold both pieces. With one piece right side up, pin lace or eyelet along the outer edge so that it is inside the seam line.

Place the second piece on top of this with the right side down. Pin together, and stitch around the edge, leaving a small opening at the neck to turn to the right side. Blind-stitch closed.

Trim designs
Bow collar: Trace and transfer the design

around the edge of the collar approximately ¾ inch from the top. Trace a small script initial (Alphabet 8, pages 59–60) on each side. Use two different colors to embroider the bow, one darker than the other for shading.

Use a satin stitch for the ribbon and a running stitch for the small letters. The colors used here are aqua and dark blue.

Tulip collar: Trace and transfer the tulip design, or choose another small pattern for the collar area. Position the initial (Alphabet 8, page 60) on the opposite side.

The tulips are embroidered with yellow and orange floss; the stems and leaves with green floss. The initial is also green.

Cherry collar: This design takes less time to create than the others because it is done with fabric crayons. Trace, then color the cherries and leaves with red and green crayons. Turn the design over, and position it on the collar. Place a piece of plain paper (such as typing paper) over the design, and press it with a medium-hot iron. The design will transfer to the collar.

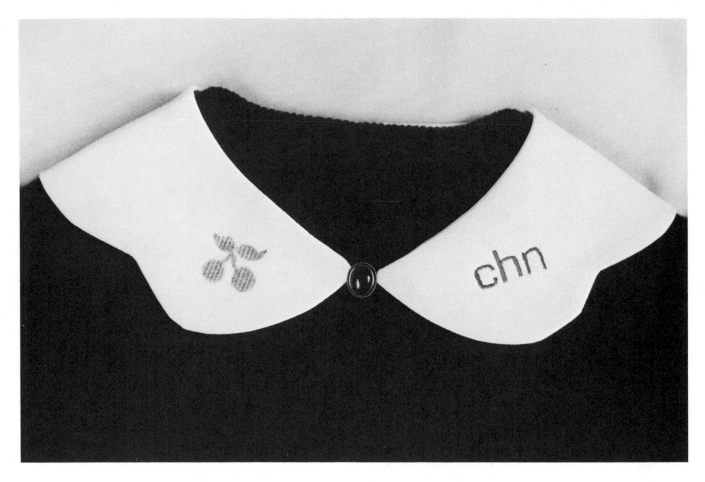

Trace and transfer your initials (Alphabet 26, page 160), and satin-stitch item with two strands of floss. The center initial is cherry red, and the other two are green.

Finish

The collars can be attached to a sweater, tacking here and there so they can be removed for laundering. If you want to change them with different outfits, they will lie on top of the sweater neck. Make a closure of a ribbon tie, or add your own pin.

Variations

Make old-fashioned lace collars with satin underlinings. If the lace is too delicate to embroider, add an initial appliqué.

Gift wrap ideas

For the cherry collar, repeat the crayon design on plain wrapping paper. Tie a few artificial cherries under a red satin bow. Re-create the bow from the collar, using the same color ribbon on the package.

For the tulip collar, add a real or artificial yellow flower to the wrap.

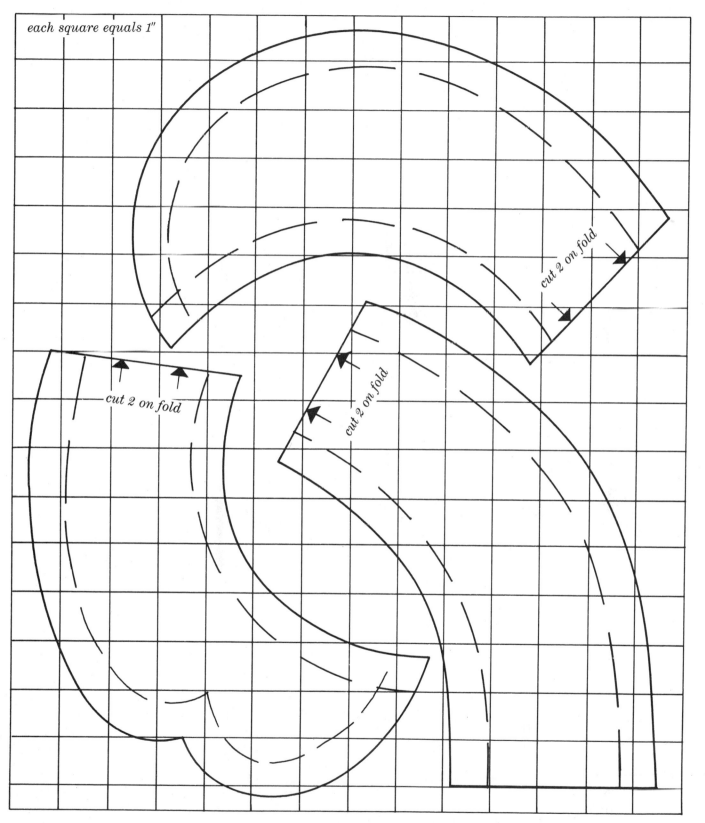

each square equals 1"

cut 2 on fold

cut 2 on fold

cut 2 on fold

159

abcdefghijklmnopqrstuvwxyz

ABCDEFGHIJKLMNOPQRSTUVWXY

abcdefghijklmnopqrstuvwxyz

abcdefghijklmnopqrstuvwxyz

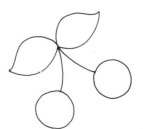

Something old, something new

Old lace, pieces of satin, ribbons, embroidered appliqués conjure up romance. Search out such scraps from the sewing basket, thrift shops, antiques and seconds stores to turn into sachets, lingerie cases, evening bags, collars and a little bag to carry down the aisle. Look for pretty cocktail napkins, coasters, lace medallions, etc.

The following bags were made from just such scraps. The "M" purse is made of satin, and the "K" initialed purse is made from two cocktail napkins and a lace medallion.

Materials needed for the satin bag

Piece of satin 5 × 12 inches; lace medallion or coaster; ⅛-inch-wide satin ribbon; embroidered appliqués; needle; thread.

Directions for the satin bag

With the right sides together, fold the satin in half lengthwise. Stitch up the sides. Fold and stitch the top hem. Sew half the lace to the back, and fold over to form a flap on the front. Sew satin ribbon around the edge of the lace, or if possible, weave it in and out.

Create an initial with the ribbon, and stitch it to the lace. Tack appliqués here and there. Add a ribbon handle, and tie it with a bow at the side. Tack in place.

Materials needed for the napkin purse

2 pink scallop-edged napkins; lace medallion or coaster; ¼-inch-wide satin ribbon; appliqués; embroidery floss; tracing paper; pencil.

Directions for the napkin purse

Pin the two pieces of fabric together with the ribbon and stitch up both sides and across the bottom edge. The lace medallion is stitched to the back and forms a closure. Tack appliqués and

ribbon to the finished bag. This bag measures 4½ × 8 inches.

Embroidery

Alphabet 27 is an old Victorian design. It is romantic in feeling and goes with this project. Trace and enlarge the initial (see page 162), and transfer it to the lower right corner. Use two strands of embroidery floss and an outline stitch to embroider the one large initial.

Variations

Use your imagination when putting a little bag together. Add ribbons, appliqués and lace trimmings of your choice. If you can't find old lace and doilies to use, buy new ones. You need so little material that the cost will be pennies.

Satin and lace pouch

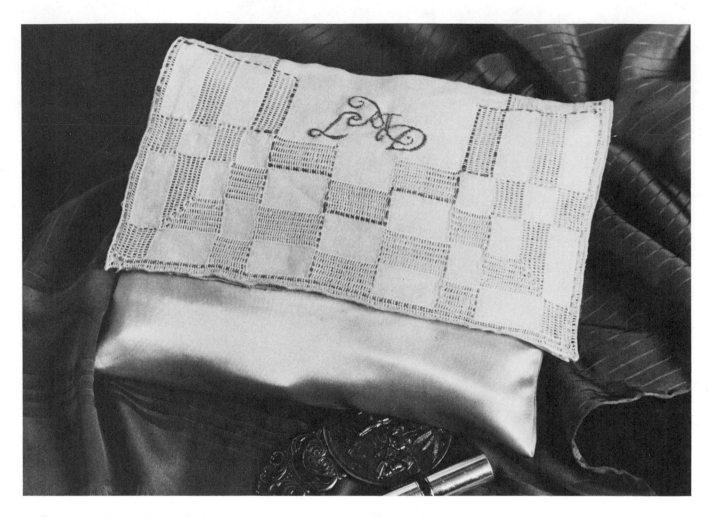

Once again satin and lace scraps are put together to create a soft and romantic pouch. This bag is made from one piece of satin and an old lace table runner. Use it to hold stockings or jewelry when you travel or as an evening bag.

Materials needed

1 piece of satin 10 × 16 inches; 1 piece of lacy fabric or organdy 6 × 10 inches; embroidery floss; embroidery hoop; needle; thread; tracing paper; pencil; ribbon (optional).

Directions

Fold the satin in half lengthwise, and stitch up both sides to create a pocket. Fold and stitch the top edge to the inside. If necessary, turn and finish the exposed edges of the lace or organdy. Stitch one edge to the back edge of the bag, and turn to the front, forming a closing flap.

Decorate the lace or organdy with embroidery floss woven in and out, or stitch decorative ribbon to edges.

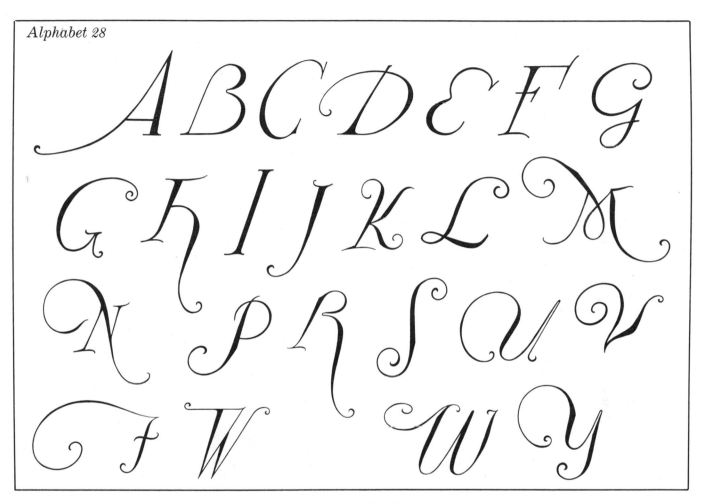

Alphabet 28

A B C D E F G
G H I J K L M
N P R S U V
F W W Y

Embroidery

The script alphabet (on this page) is light and flows together to create a pretty design. Begin by tracing your initials so they look well together. Transfer the monogram to an area of your bag that is free of decoration. Use an embroidery hoop to keep the sheer fabric taut. Do not pull thread tightly. Use one or two strands and a satin stitch for the heavier lines, an outline stitch where the lines are thinner.

Variation

Turn this bag into a small pillow by adding polyester or cotton stuffing. Stitch the top edge closed, and add lace to the front.

Gift wrap idea

Create the pouch to be the gift package for a beautiful piece of lingerie. Add a tiny bottle of perfume. Use lots of layers of tissue and a narrow satin ribbon around the outside, but no box. The whole presentation will be soft and cloudlike.

Sewing kits

A little roll-up sewing kit holds all the essentials for a quick repair job: a few spools of thread, needles and scissors.

Though utilitarian, this item takes on a gift quality when it is made of satin or velvet and is trimmed with decorative ribbon. It makes a good stocking stuffer or going-away gift for the traveler or college-bound person.

Materials needed

¼ yard of fabric (velvet used here); ¼ yard of quilted fabric for lining; 2¼ yards of ribbon; ½ yard of ¼-inch-wide elastic; scissors; needle; thread; embroidery floss; cover-your-own button size 45 (1⅛ inch); scrap piece of contrasting material to cover button; pins.

Directions

Cut one piece of velvet 18½ × 4½ inches. Cut the lining piece the same size. Cut a piece of elastic 8½ inches long. Measure 10 inches up from one end of the lining and pin elastic to both

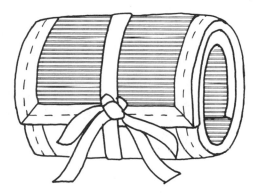

sides at this point. Pin elastic at 1-inch intervals on the lining. Stitch the elastic to the lining where it is pinned.

Cut a 1¼-inch piece of elastic and another 1½ inches long. Form two rings by sewing the ends of each piece together. Center the two elastic rings on the lining 2½ inches below the elastic strip, leaving a 1-inch space between the rings. Sew the ends of the rings to the lining.

Pin the wrong side of the lining to the wrong side of the velvet. Finish the lower edge with decorative ribbon. Fold up 2¾ inches from bottom to form a pocket. Pin in place.

Finish off the raw edges of the kit with ribbon on both sides. Stitch as close to the inside edge as possible. Roll up the sewing kit, and find the center of the flap for closure.

Make a ribbon loop long enough to fit over the button, and sew the ends together on the underside of the flap.

Embroidered button

Place the button on a scrap of fabric, and draw a circle around it. Your initial must fit within this area. Transfer the letter (Alphabet 8, page 60), and embroider it by hand or machine with a contrasting thread. Cover the button, and attach it to the sewing kit just under the ribbon loop.

Variations

This little kit can be made in a variety of fabrics, and the embroidered initial can be applied right to the front. Choose a fabric that is easier to embroider than velvet, and tie it with a decorative ribbon that is attached to the back and drawn around to either end. (See drawing.)

Gift wrap idea

Before wrapping, insert small spools of thread under elastic. Place embroidery scissors through large and small rings of elastic, and insert a few needles. The whole kit will fit in to a jewelry box. Use the matching decorative ribbon or rickrack trim to tie the package.

Make a flower on the top of the box with cutout felt petals and a center of one large button. Use rickrack for the stem. Or consider wrapping the box with bright-colored paper and creating the person's initial by glueing buttons to the top. Use tiny white shirt buttons or baby beads.

168

Sewing or jewelry box

Don't throw out those old cookie tins, margarine tubs and plastic containers. Would you believe this beautiful sewing box, which can also be used for jewelry, was once an old tin used to hold nails? All it takes is a little fabric and stuffing, and with the added charm of lace and embroidered initials, you'll have a beautiful gift for yourself or another.

Materials needed

A metal tin with lid 7½ inches around and 3½ inches high; enough fabric to cover lid; corresponding fabric for the inside, outside and both bottoms; 1 yard of 1-inch-wide pregathered lace; 7-inch circle of cardboard; polyester stuffing; scissors; needle; thread; tracing paper; pencil; embroidery floss, embroidery hoop; pins.

Directions

Cut a rectangle of fabric for the bottom sides of the tin 13 × 26½ inches. With the right sides together, stitch the short ends with a ¼-inch seam. Turn ¼ inch of one edge of the circle of fabric to the wrong side, and stitch while gathering thread to draw the circle closed; this will fit over the bottom of the can. Stuff the sides of the can between the fabric and the material. Smooth the stuffing around with a pencil or butter knife so it isn't lumpy.

Tuck the remaining fabric into the inside of the can. Cut a 9-inch circle; stitch and gather it around the edge; fit this over the cardboard circle. Alternative: Spread rubber cement on the cardboard and back of fabric. Let it dry. Smooth the fabric over the cardboard, and tape it to the underside. Whichever way you cover the bottom, set it in place in the can.

Finishing top lid

Cut a circle of fabric 17 inches around. Find the center of the circle and mark it with a pin. Enlarge the letters (Alphabet 29, page 171) you will be embroidering on the top of the sewing box. Use an embroidery hoop, and stitch each letter with three strands of floss, using the satin stitch.

Turn a ¼-inch hem around the edge of the circle, and with needle and thread loosely gather it, but do not knot the end of the thread. Be sure there is about 12 inches of unused thread in the needle.

Pad the top of the lid with stuffing, and fit the embroidered cover over the top. Tighten the gathered stitches so the lid fabric fits securely.

Stitch the pregathered lace to the fabric all the way around the bottom rim. Set the top down over the edge of the lace.

Variation

This project was made with polished cotton chintz of two different patterns. However, you can use leftover scraps to make a patchwork sewing or jewelry box.

Gift wrap idea

If this is to be a sewing box, rather than to hold jewelry, fill it with all the necessary ingredients for a well-stocked sewing container. Present it in a tissue-lined hat box with an extravagant satin bow.

abcdefg
hijklmn
opqrrst
uvwxyz

Floral place setting

This project looks as if it took hours of work and a lot of talent. Actually, like most of the projects in the book, it can be made in less than an hour, and the design is transferred and filled in with fabric markers. It's as easy as crayoning in a coloring book. The combination of the linen material, the integrated design and initials and the colors makes this an elegant way to set your table. Imagine several of them with a centerpiece of flowers to match the colors used in the designs. The personalized napkins balance the whole setting.

Materials needed

1 yard beige linen for four place mats and four napkins; thread; iron-on pencil; tracing paper; pencil; a variety of fabric or permanent markers (pink, green and brown used here); fabric protector such as Scotchgard; scissors.

Directions

Measure and cut out each rectangle, leaving enough material for a ¼-inch hem all around. Use the leftover material to make napkins. The width of your material will determine how large the napkins can be. The one shown here is 6½ inches square when folded.

If necessary, enlarge, then transfer the floral design with iron-on pencil (see pages 21–22). This method will work best for this project because the outline, once filled with color, will wash out, leaving no trace of the transfer outline, but it will be visible on the material as you work. If you can use the same size of initials shown here, trace the combination of your letters from Alphabet 30, page 174. If they must first be enlarged, see page 20.

Hold the tracing of your initials in position on the fabric to be sure they fit in the designated space. Remove the tracing, and retrace the letters on the back on the paper with the iron-on pencil. Place this on the fabric, and iron to transfer.

Applying markers

Use a scrap piece of linen to test paint or markers on your material to see the effect. (See page 27 for tips on using fabric markers.)

Carefully color the design within the transfer outline. You can use darker shades of the pink and green for accents and shading. For this project the stems are dark green, the leaves are a lighter green and the flowers and buds are bright pink. The initials must be done with more care because the lines are quite narrow. They are colored with brown marker. A magnifying glass might be helpful for checking the work as you go along.

The corner of the napkin sports a repeat of one flower in a smaller version, and the initials are the same size as those used on the place mat. When the paint is dry, the colors are permanent and the items can be washed as you would wash them if they had no design.

Variations

This design can be crewel-embroidered with excellent results. However, you might want to alter it by eliminating part of the pattern, perhaps only using the lower stem and flowers, to lessen the work involved.

Gift wrap idea

If you have a friend who enjoys craftwork, or you're visiting one in the hospital, you can make this project as a kit to present as a gift. Cut and hem the place mats and napkins. Enlarge the floral design and your friend's initials as described above. Transfer each item and give it all with the markers for the person to complete.

ABCDEFG
HIJKLMNO
PQRSTUV
WXYZ

Dear Craftworkers:

I always enjoy hearing from the people who are doing my projects, designing new things, finding new ways to do the old techniques or who have questions about crafting in general. Readers' reactions enable me to continue to design projects that are the most appealing and to let everyone know what's popular in all parts of the country.

The best information that I receive is the tips and shortcuts for doing things better, which I've been able to pass along. Sometimes I receive a snapshot of a successful project, which is a lot of fun because I can see how someone else did the same project that I made. Sometimes it will have a little twist on the original idea which leads me to say, "Now why didn't I think of that!"

So if in the course of your crafting you want to share an idea, an interesting experience or ask a question, please drop me a note.

Leslie Linsley

Nantucket

Massachusetts 02554